P9-AFK-220

tahini and turmeric

FROM TOP TO BOTTOM:
FRIED EGGPLANT, PEPPER,
AND PICKLE CHUTNEY;
ROASTED EGGPLANT COINS
WITH SILAN, POMEGRANATES,
AND PISTACHIOS; AND
SPICY TOMATO AND PEPPER JAM

tahini and turmeric

 101 MIDDLE EASTERN CLASSICS—MADE IRRESISTIBLY VEGAN

vicky cohen and ruth fox

Da Capo

LIFE
LONG

Da Capo Lifelong Books

Da Capo Press
Hachette Book Group
1290 Avenue of the Americas,
New York, NY 10104
www.dacapopress.com
@DaCapoPress

Printed in Canada

First Edition: May 2018

Published by Da Capo Press, an imprint of Perseus Books, LLC,
a subsidiary of Hachette Book Group, Inc. The Da Capo Press name and logo is a trademark of the Hachette Book Group.

The Hachette Speakers Bureau provides a wide range of authors for speaking events. To find out more, go to www.hachettespeakersbureau.com or call (866) 376-6591.

The publisher is not responsible for websites (or their content) that are not owned by the publisher.

Print book interior design by Nancy Singer.

Library of Congress Cataloging-in-Publication Data

Names: Cohen, Vicky, 1967- author. | Fox, Ruth, 1977- author. Title: Tahini and turmeric : 101 Middle Eastern classics—made irresistibly vegan / by Vicky Cohen and Ruth Fox. Description: First edition. | Boston : Da Capo Lifelong Books, 2018. Identifiers: LCCN 2017045662 (print) | LCCN 2017046622 (ebook) | ISBN 9780738220116 (ebook) | ISBN 9780738220109 (hardback) Subjects: LCSH: Cooking, Middle Eastern. | Vegan cooking—Middle East. | Sephardic cooking. | BISAC: COOKING / Regional & Ethnic / Middle Eastern. | COOKING / Vegetarian & Vegan. | COOKING / Specific Ingredients / Herbs, Spices, Condiments. | LCGFT: Cookbooks.Classification: LCC TX725.M628 (ebook) | LCC TX725.M628 .C64 2018 (print) | DDC 641.5956—dc23
LC record available at https://lccn.loc.gov/2017045662

ISBNs: 978-0-7382-2010-9 (paper over board); 978-0-7382-2011-6 (e-book)

FRI

10 9 8 7 6 5 4 3 2 1

To Mami, Papi, and Abuelita, your unconditional love means the world to us. To Rebeca, our lives will never be complete until we have you here with us again. To Lee, Raquel, Zeke, and Solly, we love you always and forever.

COCONUT TURMERIC
SWEET BREAD (*SFUFF*)

contents

3

appetite teasers

4

body warmers

8

the main event

9

fresh from the oven

10

sweet endings

PANFRIED HERBED FALAFEL PATTIES

introduction

tahini, turmeric—and so much more

Creamy tahini and fragrant turmeric are just two of the enticing flavors we grew up tasting in our Jewish-Lebanese home in Barcelona. But there was so much more; whenever we think of home, the tastes of tart-sweet pomegranates, earthy za'atar, and floral orange blossom water also come to mind. In *Tahini and Turmeric*, we're delighted to share our interpretations of the classic Middle Eastern dishes we grew up with. Bold, aromatic, and all vegan, these recipes are your ticket to experience Middle Eastern flavors. If you're new to vegan cooking, these recipes will tempt you with fresh, bright ingredients and new flavors. If you're new to making Middle Eastern food at home, be ready to explore beyond the staples of baba ghanoush and baklava. Best of all, many of these dishes are meant to be served on busy weeknights and during casual gatherings with friends. We love sharing good food and good stories around the table—these are the meals we feed our own family and friends, and have also shared on our blog, mayihavethatrecipe.com. Before we get to the basics, we'd like to introduce ourselves:

vicky

When I first moved to the United States from Barcelona around twenty years ago, I could barely cook an egg. While I was growing up, my job in the kitchen was only to help our mother clean up. Mami is a speedy cook, so she didn't have time to waste teaching me the ins and outs of her recipes! She would wake at nine a.m., enjoy a cup of coffee, and finish preparing an entire holiday meal by noon.

One amazing fact about Mami is that, besides being a great cook, she is a vegetarian, but cooks the tastiest meat dishes ever, always seasoned to perfection, without tasting one little bit (I can practically see Chef Ramsay rolling his eyes right now . . .). She has a "magic" touch, I guess.

As far as I can remember, Mami has been a vegetarian. Our father, Papi, is a big meat and fish eater, but his hobby for decades has been tending our amazing fruit and vegetable garden right outside Barcelona. I've discovered that nothing elevates a dish like freshly picked produce. Stuck in my memory is a ratatouille made with fresh tomatoes, zucchini, eggplants, and peppers, bursting with so much flavor that all we needed to make it a full dinner was a hunk of crusty bread to soak up the juices. Going to the garden with Papi to pick all that juicy, flavorful produce was an even better experience. I loved going to the fig trees and picking as many ripe fruits as possible, so Mami could make dozens of jars of spiced caramelized figs.

After moving to the United States to be with my husband, I spent countless hours on the phone asking Mami for recipes, writing them down, and testing them. Her instructions were never specific: just add a little bit of this and a little bit of that; if you see it needs more water, just add some; feel the dough and see if it's the right consistency . . . as if I was supposed to know! But surprisingly, I never asked for measurements. I was so used to seeing

Mami cook without ever using a recipe that I thought everyone did it like that. (I guess all that time cleaning up was instructional after all!)

I must have had good cooking genes, because soon after, I began developing my own recipes, using the flavors and spices Mami used at home and combining them with the produce and products available here in the United States. My husband pretty much knew I had inherited those good genes, and I'm pretty sure it was one of the reasons he proposed! To this day, he talks about the five-course vegan meal Mami improvised the first time he came to our house in Barcelona for dinner.

My husband is in constant evolution: he was a vegan when I first met him; then, he became vegetarian; then he started adding meat to his diet. Right now, he eats mostly vegan and vegetarian meals with meat or fish occasionally. His diet keeps me on my toes to see how I can adapt a dish and still make it flavorful. The recipes in this book reflect my cooking evolution to bold, aromatic dishes, where vegetables are front and center, and no one misses the meat.

ruth

The very first thing I ever made in the kitchen was a red pepper vinaigrette with chopped onion and garlic. It was a Sunday afternoon, at our apartment in Barcelona, and I was bored to death. So I went into the kitchen, hoping to kill some time.

The vinaigrette had the consistency of thick soup, filled with big chunks of thick pepper skin, but I thought it was absolutely awesome. At eleven years old, I was so proud of it, and couldn't wait for my parents to try it.

The next thing I attempted was rice, for which I prepared the exact same ingredients I used for the vinaigrette. As the logical child I was, it made sense that if the ingredients tasted good together as a dressing, they also worked in a different dish. Soon after, I successfully ventured into baking, which became one of my favorite pastimes.

I've always been a big food lover, even as a child. And by *food* I don't mean desserts, candy, or junk food. I mean delicious home-cooked meals.

As much as I enjoyed eating Mami's cooking, watching her in the kitchen was one of my favorite things to do, especially during the Jewish holidays. I even looked forward to going food shopping with her, which, let's be honest, is a little odd for a kid. I wanted to help in the kitchen just as my older sister Vicky did, but Mami would only let me do the not-so-exciting stuff. That slowly started to change, however, as my sisters grew older and were no longer around as much. And once they both moved overseas, that was it: Mami granted me carte blanche.

By then, I was already a teenager who still loved food but was becoming more aware of her weight problem. Finding the balance between the two wasn't easy, but I can proudly say that I succeeded. I still enjoyed every single bite, thanks to my mom's ability to infuse flavor into whatever she makes.

Around that time, I became a vegetarian (for no noble reason, I must admit), and a few years later, motivated by my passion for food and my eagerness to help people, I got a degree in human nutrition and dietetics from the University of Barcelona.

Throughout the years, I've tried almost every diet from vegetarian to low carb, paleo vegetarian, sugar-free, and vegan, mainly to better help my clients. I was also trying to figure out what worked best for my troubled digestive system. After years of experimenting, I realized that a plant-based diet makes me feel the best.

We all know that a diet rich in fruits and veggies is beneficial for overall health. But for me, two things stood out: my energy level increased significantly (honestly, I'm not sure that's a good thing, since I'm known for not being able to sit still!); and after I cut out dairy (extremely difficult because I absolutely love it), most of my belly troubles went away.

Throughout these experiments with diet, I've made changes without sacrificing the flavors and many of the foods I grew up eating and love so much. Doing so has been the main motivation and inspiration for writing this book.

In this book, we share 101 of our favorite recipes. We'll begin by walking you through our pantry. Some of the ingredients may be new to you; we'll tell you where to get them and offer substitutions as we're able. Just as Mami encouraged us to do, we urge you to get into the kitchen, experiment, and have fun. Creating healthy, delicious dishes for yourself and your family or friends is one of the best gifts you can give. We named our blog *May I Have That Recipe?* and we're so happy to be sharing our recipes with you!

BULGUR WHEAT PIE

1

the middle eastern pantry

Many of the ingredients here will be familiar to you, but some will be new. The following are our pantry staples that you'll need for these recipes.

ALEPPO PEPPER: A fruity and slightly spicy crushed red pepper native to the city of Aleppo in Syria. Due to the civil war, it is hard to find the pepper grown in the Syrian city. However, it is being harvested in Turkey and Lebanon.

Our preferred brand: Sahadi

ALMOND FLOUR: Also called almond meal, or ground almonds. It's made from ground blanched almonds, although you can find some made with raw almonds.

Our preferred brand: Bob's Red Mill

BAHARAT: This combination of spices, such as allspice, cloves, coriander, and black pepper, is used often in Middle Eastern cuisine. Each baharat blend varies in flavor depending on the spices used. If you don't have any on hand, you can use plain ground allspice instead.

Our preferred brand: La Boîte NYC (www.laboiteny.com)

BULGUR WHEAT: This dried cracked wheat is used often in Middle Eastern cuisine. It can be used in salads such as Quinoa and Black Bean Tabbouleh (page 110) or to make a dough for Bulgur Wheat Pie (page 199). Bulgur's coarseness varies, depending on how it is ground—from #1 (fine) to #4 (very coarse). The coarse form is the one commonly found in conventional grocery stores. The fine variety can be found in Middle Eastern markets or online.

Our preferred brand: Sunnyland Mills

CARDAMOM: A spice used mainly in Indian and Middle Eastern cuisines; very fragrant, slightly flowery, and smoky. Cardamom is a pod filled with seeds, and the main varieties are black and green. It can be found whole or ground.

Our preferred brand: La Boîte NYC (www.laboiteny.com)

CHIA SEEDS: These little black seeds that resemble poppy seeds are high in fiber, omega-3, and protein. They become gelatinous once soaked in water, and are used in vegan cooking as a thickener or as a replacement for eggs.

Our preferred brand: Nutiva

CHICKPEA FLOUR: A gluten-free flour made from finely ground dried chickpeas, this is often used to replace wheat flour in gluten-free cooking, and also acts as a binder in vegan recipes.

Our preferred brand: Bob's Red Mill

COCONUT BEVERAGE: This nondairy beverage is made from the water and meat of a coconut and can be used instead of dairy milk in coffee, cereal, and so on. It can be found in the refrigerated section of most grocery stores. Note that this is different from canned coconut milk (see listing).

Our preferred brand: So Delicious

COCONUT CREAMER: A nondairy coffee creamer made from coconuts, it is thicker than coconut beverage and often sweetened and flavored. It works great as a base for vegan creams and custards.

Our preferred brand: So Delicious

COCONUT MILK: Usually sold in cans, it's a thicker, creamier liquid than coconut beverage or creamer. It has a high fat content (often the fat and liquid will separate in the can) and can be used instead of heavy cream in vegan recipes.

Our preferred brand: Native Forest

COCONUT OIL: The fat extracted from coconuts. Extra-virgin coconut oil has a predominant coconut flavor, whereas the refined oil is almost neutral. It's a great dairy-free substitute for butter, especially in baking. Unless specified, you can use extra-virgin or refined for our recipes, depending on whether you want a hint of coconut taste.

Our preferred brand: Nutiva

CORIANDER: The dried seeds of the cilantro plant, which have slight floral undertones. The seeds are sold whole or ground.

Our preferred brand: La Boîte NYC (www.laboiteny.com)

CUMIN: Sold ground or as seeds, this spice has an intense flavor and aroma that pairs very well with coriander and turmeric.

Our preferred brand: La Boîte NYC (www.laboiteny.com)

HARISSA: This wonderful, intensely flavored spicy chile paste is used in North African and Middle Eastern cuisines. It is made with dried chiles, roasted peppers, garlic, olive oil, and spices that vary from brand to brand.

Our preferred brand: Mina

KATAIFI: Shredded phyllo dough, commonly used in Greek and Middle Eastern cuisines. It comes frozen and needs to be thawed in the refrigerator. The strands are usually separated before being used.

Our preferred brand: Apollo

LEMON JUICE: You will see lemon juice mentioned very often throughout this cookbook. Make sure to use freshly squeezed, and not the kind sold in bottles in the grocery store, since the flavor is incredibly different.

NIGELLA SEEDS: Small, black seeds with an herbal flavor, usually added to breads, crackers, and other savory baked goods.

Our preferred brand: La Boîte NYC (www.laboiteny.com)

NONDAIRY MILK: A beverage that comes from plant sources, such as almond, soy, coconut, nuts, and seeds. These milks can be sweetened, unsweetened, plain, or flavored. For baking, you'll want to try unsweetened, unflavored varieties first.

Our preferred brands: So Delicious and Califia Farms

NONDAIRY YOGURT: This yogurt alternative is made from cultured nondairy milk. Popular varieties include soy, almond, coconut, and cashew. You can find unsweetened, unflavored, and sweetened and flavored varieties. As with milks, for use in recipes, first try unsweetened and unflavored, unless specified otherwise in the recipe.

Our preferred brands: So Delicious and Forager

NUTRITIONAL YEAST: Also known as "nooch," this single-celled organism, *Saccharomyces cerevisiae*, is grown on molasses and then harvested, washed, and dried with heat to "deactivate" it, so it has no leavening ability (unlike baking yeast). It tastes much better than it sounds, adding a cheeselike flavor to savory dishes. It's also a good source of vitamin B_{12} and protein.

Our preferred brand: Bob's Red Mill

OIL, NEUTRAL FLAVOR: Neutral oils are those used just for cooking (deep-frying, sautéing, baking), without adding any flavor to the food. Sunflower, grapeseed, and avocado are the ones we prefer.

ORANGE BLOSSOM WATER: A floral water with hints of orange, used in Middle Eastern and North African cuisines. It can be found easily online at Amazon.com; at larger health food stores, such as Whole Foods Market; and at Middle Eastern grocery stores.

Our preferred brands: Cortas and Sadaf

POMEGRANATE MOLASSES: Made from concentrated pomegranate juice and used extensively in Middle Eastern and Persian cuisines, it has an intense sweet-and-sour fruity flavor. It can be found easily online at Amazon.com; at larger health food stores, such as Whole Foods Market; and at Middle Eastern grocery stores.

Our preferred brands: Cortas and Sadaf

ROSE WATER: A floral water with a strong rose flavor, used in Middle Eastern and Indian cuisines. It can be found easily online at Amazon.com; at larger health food stores, such as Whole Foods Market; and at Middle Eastern grocery stores.

Our preferred brands: Cortas and Sadaf

SAFFRON: One of the most expensive spices per pound found in the market, these beautiful red, delicate threads add a luxurious, rich, and unique flavor to dishes, as well as a bright yellow-orange color. It is used in small amounts.

Our preferred brand: La Boîte NYC (www.laboiteny.com)

SEMOLINA FLOUR: A coarse flour made from durum wheat, it's traditionally used to make pasta and couscous. In Middle Eastern cuisine, it is used in desserts, and also as a thickener in soups.

SILAN: Also called date honey or date syrup, it's a sweet, dark syrup made by boiling dates and water until concentrated. We prefer to use the silan that is made without any added sugar. It can be found easily online at Amazon.com; at larger health food stores, such as Whole Foods Market; and at Middle Eastern grocery stores.

Our preferred brand: Oxygen

SUMAC: This reddish, lemony-tasting spice is made from ground red berries of the nonpoisonous sumac plant.

Our preferred brand: La Boîte NYC (www.laboiteny.com)

SWEET PAPRIKA: A mild, deep red spice that gives dishes a slightly fruity flavor.

Our preferred brand: Pereg Gourmet

TAHINI: This thick, nutty paste is made from ground sesame seeds. It has the same consistency as other nut and seed butters.

Our preferred brand: Soom

TEMPEH: Tempeh is a plant-based meat substitute made from fermented soy, grains, and sometimes beans. It's high in protein, fiber, and probiotics, and it can be prepared in many different ways. It can sometimes have a slightly bitter taste when it's cooked, but that can be avoided by boiling it, steaming it, or soaking it in hot water before cooking it. Tempeh has a great meaty texture and not a very strong taste, so it pretty much absorbs the taste of the ingredients it is cooked with.

Our preferred brand: Trader Joe's

TURMERIC POWDER: Also known as ground turmeric, this bright, yellow spice commonly used in Middle Eastern and Indian cuisines has a very distinctive taste and a beautiful golden color.

Our preferred brand: Pereg Gourmet

VEGAN MAYO: A spread made from oil, lemon juice or vinegar, and salt. It is used like traditional mayonnaise, has a very similar texture and taste, and can be found in most grocery stores.

Our preferred brand: Hampton Creek

VITAL WHEAT GLUTEN: This is the protein found in wheat. It comes in a powder, flourlike form, and it's the base for seitan, a meat substitute. You can find it in natural grocery stores or online.

Our preferred brand: Arrowhead Mills

WHEAT BERRIES: Wheat berries are whole wheat kernels with a wonderful nutty taste and chewy texture. They are high in protein and fiber, and rich in B vitamins and minerals. They are a great base for hearty salads and soups.

Our preferred brand: Bob's Red Mill

WHOLE WHEAT PASTRY FLOUR: This fine, soft whole wheat flour is ideal for baking. It has a milder flavor and lighter consistency than regular whole wheat flour.

Our preferred brand: Bob's Red Mill

ZA'ATAR: A Middle Eastern staple, this condiment is made from a combination of dried wild thyme, sesame seeds, dried sumac, and salt. It can be found at Middle Eastern stores, and online at Amazon.com.

grocery list

We've compiled this list for you—copy it or take a picture with your phone and use it as a checklist when you go shopping.

nondairy milks
almond milk
cashew milk
coconut creamer
coconut milk beverage
soy milk

oils
coconut oil
neutral-flavor oil: sunflower, avocado, grapeseed
olive oil

jarred/canned goods
artichoke bottoms
canned pure pumpkin puree
cannellini beans
chickpeas (a.k.a. garbanzo beans)
coconut milk
crushed tomatoes
fava beans
hearts of palm
hot cherry peppers
pickles
roasted red peppers
stuffed grape leaves
sun-dried tomatoes, packed in oil
tahini
tomato paste
tomato puree

condiments
agave nectar
beet powder
harissa
mushroom broth
mustard: dijon, whole-grain, spicy brown
orange blossom water
pomegranate juice
pomegranate molasses
pure maple syrup
pure vanilla extract
rose water
silan (a.k.a. date honey or date syrup)
vegan mayo
vegetable broth
vinegar: balsamic, red wine

flour, rice, and other dry staples
active dry yeast
all-purpose flour
almond flour
baking powder
baking soda
basmati rice
bread flour
bulgur wheat
chickpea (garbanzo) flour
confectioners' sugar

farro
granulated sugar
israeli couscous
jasmine rice
light brown sugar
old-fashioned rolled oats
polenta
quinoa
salt: sea salt, coarse salt
self-rising flour
semolina flour
spelt flour
unsweetened cocoa powder
unsweetened shredded coconut
vermicelli noodles
vital wheat gluten
wheat berries
whole wheat couscous
whole wheat panko bread crumbs
whole wheat pastry flour
wild rice

dried beans
black beans
cannellini beans
chickpeas
lentils: french green, black beluga, red

nuts and seeds
almonds
cashews
chestnuts, roasted
chia seeds
flaxseeds: whole, ground

pecans
pine nuts
pistachios
pumpkin seeds
sesame seeds: black, white
sunflower seeds
walnuts

herbs and spices

fresh
cilantro
dill
mint
parsley
rosemary

dried
aleppo pepper
allspice, ground
aniseeds
baharat
black pepper, freshly ground
caraway seeds
cardamom, ground
chili powder
cinnamon, ground
cloves, ground
coriander, ground
coriander seeds
cumin, ground
fennel seeds
garlic powder
nigella seeds
onion powder
oregano, dried
paprika: sweet, hot
pumpkin pie spice
saffron

sumac
thyme, dried
turmeric, ground
za'atar

vegetables
beets
bell peppers: red, green,
    orange, yellow
carrots
cauliflower
celery
celery root (a.k.a. celeriac)
corn kernels
cucumber
eggplants
endives
garlic
jalapeño peppers
leeks
lettuce
mushrooms: portobello,
    shiitake, baby bella
    (cremini), chanterelle,
    baby oyster
okra
onions
parsnips
potatoes
radishes
rutabaga
scallions
shallots
spinach
squash: spaghetti,
    butternut, delicata
sweet potatoes
tomatoes

turnips
yellow summer squash
zucchini

fruit
apricots, dried
avocados
bananas
cherries: fresh, dried
cranberries, dried
figs: fresh, dried
lemons
medjool dates
olives: kalamata, black cured
orange juice
oranges
persimmons
pomegranates
prunes
raisins

protein
tempeh
tofu
vegan sausage

other items
kataifi
nondairy yogurt
nutritional yeast
pita bread: plain, whole wheat
spring roll wrappers
vegan chocolate chips
vegan country bread
vegan crescent roll dough
vegan mayo
vegan puff pastry
vegetable bouillon

TAHINI SMOOTHIE BOWL

2

day starters and brunch nosh

This is how we do the most important meal of the day, Middle Eastern style. Heavy bagels and sugary cereals, be gone! These breakfast and brunch recipes might not be what you're used to, but they will sure leave your belly full and your body energized. Once you try them, you'll kiss your traditional morning routine good-bye.

When we visit Israel, we love to go to breakfast at fancy hotels, which serve endless buffets of fresh salads, *shakshukas* (egg dishes), dips, spreads, and puffy pitas. The recipes in this chapter are inspired by our hours of enjoyment in their dining rooms, hanging out with family and stuffing ourselves with such delicious food.

Overnight Oats with Cardamom
and Pistachios
13

Turmeric, Apricot, and
Pistachio Granola
15

Tahini Smoothie Bowl
19

Chickpea and Pepper Shakshuka
20

Spicy Avocado Toast with Dukkah
23

Za'atar Pita Toast with
Avocado and Tomato
25

Zucchini Fritters with Cucumber
Yogurt Sauce
26

Falafel Waffles
29

Mini Spinach Pies with
Pine Nuts and
Dried Cherries
31

Cashew Ricotta Stuffed Syrian
Pancakes with Orange Blossom
Syrup (*Atayef*)
35

Nutty Cinnamon Rolls with
Halvah Icing
37

overnight oats with cardamom and pistachios

Of all the stories and memories we collected while growing up, the funniest are those involving our dad. Papi's one of those people who can make us laugh without even trying. Each September, he would harvest pomegranates from our garden, spending most of the evening peeling and seeding them in the living room while watching TV. That drove our mom crazy, even though she always stole a few handfuls to add to her bowl of honey, cinnamon, and cardamom oatmeal (yes, our mom eats oatmeal for dinner!). We started making overnight oats a couple of years ago, and we love this combination of flavors inspired by our childhood memories. Sweet and creamy, with the freshness of the pomegranate seeds, crunch from the pistachios, and a hint of exotic cardamom, this satisfying breakfast takes fifteen minutes to prepare at night and will be ready for you when you wake up—or, if you're like our mom, before bed!

Prep time: 15 minutes
Makes 2 servings

INGREDIENTS:

1 cup old-fashioned rolled oats

2 tablespoons chia seeds

¼ teaspoon ground cardamom

⅛ teaspoon salt

2 cups unsweetened nondairy milk, lukewarm (this helps the maple syrup dissolve better)

3 tablespoons pure maple syrup

1 cup fresh pomegranate seeds

1 Fuyu persimmon, cut in half, seeded, and sliced

⅓ cup shelled pistachios, roughly chopped

Combine the oats, chia seeds, cardamom, and salt in a large bowl.

In a separate bowl, combine the nondairy milk and maple syrup, and stir well until the maple syrup dissolves. Pour the liquid over the oat mixture and mix well.

Arrange one quarter of the pomegranate seeds, persimmon slices, and pistachios at the bottom of each of two containers. Top each with one quarter of the oat mixture. Repeat the process until the jars are full. Cover the jars and refrigerate overnight.

HOW TO PEEL A POMEGRANATE

Score the pomegranate horizontally down the middle. Gently twist both sides to separate the halves. Fill a large bowl with water. Hold one of the pomegranate halves in your hand, cut side down, over the bowl and tap the fruit's thick skin with a wooden spoon. The arils will fall out into the bowl, and the little pieces of yellow skin will come to the surface, so they can be easily removed. Repeat the process with the other half.

turmeric, apricot, and pistachio granola

If you've never made granola at home, you'll be surprised how incredibly easy it is to prepare. It's far cheaper and healthier—but the best part? You can make it your own by using your favorite spices, nuts, seeds, and dried fruit! There's just one thing you must remember: bake it low and slow, stirring it often (especially toward the end), to make sure it cooks evenly and doesn't burn. You would be amazed how quickly it can go from barely ready to burnt to a crisp!

This recipe includes two of our favorite combinations: turmeric-coconut-tahini, and apricot-pistachio. You will see those often throughout this book! Feel free to experiment with your own favorite combinations.

Store the cooled granola in an airtight container for up to two weeks.

Prep time: 10 minutes
Cook time: 45 minutes
Makes 4 cups

INGREDIENTS:

1½ cups old-fashioned rolled oats

½ cup unsweetened shredded coconut

¼ cup raw pumpkin seeds

2 tablespoons black sesame seeds

2 teaspoons ground turmeric

1 teaspoon ground cinnamon

1 teaspoon pumpkin pie spice

⅛ teaspoon coarse salt

⅓ cup pure maple syrup

3 tablespoons coconut oil, melted

2 tablespoons tahini

1 teaspoon pure vanilla extract

½ cup dried apricots, chopped small

⅓ cup roasted shelled pistachios

EQUIPMENT:

Parchment paper

Preheat the oven to 275°F. Line a large baking sheet with parchment paper and set aside.

Combine the oats, coconut, pumpkin and sesame seeds, turmeric, cinnamon, pumpkin pie spice, and salt in a large bowl and mix well.

In a separate bowl, whisk together the maple syrup, melted coconut oil, tahini, and vanilla. Pour the liquid over the oat mixture and mix well, so all the dry ingredients are well coated with the wet. (Using your hands is the best way to accomplish this! You can rub your hands with a little coconut oil to keep them from getting too sticky.)

Spread the mixture on the lined baking sheet in a single, even layer and bake for 42 to 45 minutes, stirring every 15 minutes so it bakes evenly, until golden brown. Remove from the oven, let cool completely, then transfer the mixture to a large bowl. Add the chopped apricots and pistachios and toss well.

tahini smoothie bowl

This recipe has everything you need to start your day: hearty and fiber-rich oats; healthy fats to keep you satisfied; and dates, silan (date syrup), and fruit to keep you energized. The tahini adds creaminess and a wonderful nutty taste that complements the freshness of the fruit beautifully. During the colder months, when figs and cherries are not available, you can use diced persimmon, pomegranate seeds, and chopped pistachios instead.

Prep time: 5 minutes
Makes 1 bowl

INGREDIENTS:

½ cup unsweetened nondairy milk

3 Medjool dates, pitted

2 tablespoons tahini

⅓ cup old-fashioned rolled oats

10 ice cubes, or to taste

TOPPINGS:

4 cherries, pitted and halved

2 fresh figs, sliced

1 teaspoon silan (date syrup; see note below)

Combine the milk, dates, tahini, and oats in a blender and blend until smooth. Add the ice and continue to blend until thick and frothy.

Transfer the smoothie to a medium-size bowl, top with the cherries and figs, and drizzle with the silan.

note: If you don't have silan, you can use maple syrup—just be aware that the flavor will change significantly.

chickpea and pepper shakshuka

Every year, our great-uncle Robert would visit us from Israel. He loved Barcelona, touring the city and the surrounding beach towns, and he would often take us with him on his daily excursions. One of his favorite dishes was *shakshuka*; one of our fondest memories of him is waking up to the delicious smell of the garlicky, rich tomato sauce, ready to be soaked up with crunchy, crusty fresh bread. Our version of this Israeli breakfast uses chickpeas rather than eggs as the main source of protein; slices of cooked polenta add creaminess and make it visually similar to the traditional recipe.

Prep time: 10 minutes
Cook time: 50 minutes
Makes 4 servings

INGREDIENTS:

2 tablespoons plus 2 teaspoons
   extra-virgin olive oil

1 large sweet onion, thinly sliced

1 red bell pepper, seeded and diced

1 orange bell pepper, seeded
   and diced

1 yellow bell pepper, seeded
   and diced

1 teaspoon sweet paprika

½ teaspoon ground cumin

¼ teaspoon ground coriander

6 slices precooked polenta
   (sold in a tube)

1 (28-ounce) can crushed tomatoes

1 (15-ounce) can chickpeas

½ cup chopped fresh cilantro, plus a
   little bit more for garnish

2 garlic cloves, crushed

¾ teaspoon salt

½ teaspoon Aleppo pepper

TIME-SAVING TIP

The *shakshuka* base can be prepared 2 or 3 days ahead of time and kept refrigerated. It can also be frozen for up to a month. When ready to serve, bring to a simmer, add the polenta slices, and continue simmering for 5 minutes.

Heat 2 tablespoons of the olive oil in a 12-inch nonstick skillet with a lid. Add the onion, bell peppers, paprika, cumin, and coriander and cook, uncovered, over medium-low heat, stirring often, for 30 minutes, or until the peppers are tender.

In the meantime, heat the remaining 2 teaspoons of olive oil in a separate large, nonstick skillet. Add the polenta slices and cook over medium heat for 1 minute, or until they brown lightly. Carefully flip the slices, then cook them for another minute. Remove from the heat and set aside.

Add the tomatoes, chickpeas, cilantro, crushed garlic, salt, and Aleppo pepper to the bell pepper mixture. Cover the skillet and continue to cook for another 15 minutes, or until the sauce starts to reduce.

Carefully arrange the polenta slices over the tomato mixture and simmer, covered, for 5 minutes.

Serve warm with crusty bread.

SPICY AVOCADO TOAST
WITH DUKKAH

spicy avocado toast with dukkah

We absolutely love avocado toast; it's so versatile, we could serve it at every single meal and not get tired of it! Out of all the toppings we have used for our avo-toast, these are some of our favorites: the sweetness of the beets is complemented by the creamy, rich avocado; topped off with *dukkah* (a spicy nut blend). It's an irresistibly savory combo.

Prep time: 10 minutes
Cook time: 1 hour 5 minutes
Makes 2 toasts

INGREDIENTS:

1 beet, thoroughly washed

1 Hass avocado, peeled and pitted

1 to 1½ tablespoons freshly squeezed lemon juice

¼ teaspoon salt

¼ teaspoon Aleppo pepper

2 slices vegan whole-grain country bread, toasted

2 teaspoons Dukkah (page 130)

Sriracha or hot sauce, for drizzling

Preheat the oven to 400°F. Wrap the beet in aluminum foil, place on a baking sheet, and roast in the oven for 1 hour, or until tender. Remove from the oven; once it's cool enough to handle safely, remove the skin and slice the beet thinly. Set aside.

To prepare the toast, mash the avocado in a small bowl with the lemon juice and salt. Add the Aleppo pepper and mix well. Spread over the two slices of toasted bread and top with sliced beet. Sprinkle with the *dukkah* and drizzle sriracha or hot sauce on top.

notes: Other topping combinations we love to add to the mashed avocado are roasted eggplant with pome-granate seeds and sesame seeds; sliced tomatoes with a sprinkle of za'atar, sliced cucumber, cured olives, and toasted pine nuts. You can even go the sweet route, with sliced bananas, a drizzle of silan, and cacao nibs.

TIME-SAVING TIP
Prepare the roasted beet ahead of time, or buy precooked ones at the grocery store.

za'atar pita toast with avocado and tomato

Za'atar is a Middle Eastern herb combo of dried wild thyme, sumac, and sesame seeds; it has a very complex, rich flavor, with a distinctive tartness that hits you at the end. When we were kids, za'atar was pretty much our peanut butter and jelly. Our mom would make us za'atar pita sandwiches to take to school, and our friends would always beg us for a piece, or would ask us to trade their pastries for our sandwich. Nowadays, we sprinkle it on salads and soups to add a little tang and enhance the flavor. But our favorite way to eat it is mixed with olive oil and spread on pita, fresh bread, or pizza dough.

Prep time: 5 minutes
Cook time: 7 minutes
Makes 4 pita toasts

INGREDIENTS:

¼ cup za'atar

2 tablespoons extra-virgin olive oil

2 whole wheat pita breads, opened and separated along the edge into 4 disks

24 cherry or grape tomatoes, sliced in half

2 Persian cucumbers, sliced

1 Hass avocado, peeled, pitted, and sliced

Preheat the oven to 375°F. Line a large baking sheet with aluminum foil.

Combine the za'atar and olive oil in a small bowl and stir well, using a spoon. Spread the mixture on the inner side of each pita disk.

Transfer the pita disks to the lined baking sheet and bake for 7 minutes. Remove from the oven, let cool slightly, and top each toast with tomato, cucumber, and avocado slices.

zucchini fritters with cucumber yogurt sauce

One of our childhood favorites was *hajet kusah*, which translates literally to "zucchini omelet." Our mom's recipe was made from shredded zucchini and feta cheese mixed with beaten eggs and baked in the oven, served with yogurt sauce. Our vegan version omits the eggs and cheese, and uses chickpea flour and vegan mayo as a binder. And the sauce? A simple swap of coconut or cashew yogurt and we've made the same tangy cucumber dressing.

It's very important to squeeze as much water as possible from the shredded zucchini, to keep the batter from being too watery. Store the fritters and the sauce in the refrigerator in separate airtight containers for up to four days.

Prep time: 15 minutes
Cook time: 30 minutes
Makes 15 fritters

INGREDIENTS:

3 to 4 medium-size zucchini, thoroughly washed and shredded unpeeled (about 5 cups)

3 to 4 medium-size carrots, peeled and shredded (about 2 cups)

¾ cup chopped fresh parsley

1 teaspoon garlic powder

1 teaspoon ground turmeric

1 teaspoon salt

¼ teaspoon freshly ground black pepper

1 cup chickpea flour

½ cup vegan mayo

⅓ cup grapeseed or avocado oil

YOGURT SAUCE:

½ cup plain unsweetened coconut or cashew yogurt

1½ teaspoons freshly squeezed lemon juice

¼ teaspoon salt

1 small cucumber, peeled and cut into small dice

EQUIPMENT:

Parchment paper

Preheat the oven to 350°F and line a baking sheet with parchment paper.

Using a piece of cheesecloth or a clean kitchen towel and working with 1 cup at a time, wring the excess water from the shredded zucchini.

Transfer to a large bowl, add the shredded carrot, parsley, garlic powder, turmeric, salt, and pepper and mix well. Add the chickpea flour and vegan mayo and mix until well combined.

Heat the oil in a large, nonstick skillet over medium heat. Scoop ¼ cup of the mixture into the hot oil, carefully flattening it with the back of a spatula. Repeat with as many scoops as will fit, being careful not to crowd the pan. Cook over medium-high heat, 2 to 3 minutes per side, or until golden brown. Repeat the process with the rest of the batter.

Transfer the fritters to the lined baking sheet and bake for 15 minutes.

To prepare the yogurt sauce, whisk together the yogurt, lemon juice, and salt. Add the diced cucumber and mix well. Refrigerate until you're ready to use it.

Serve the fritters topped with the sauce or with the sauce on the side.

falafel waffles

If you love falafel as we do, you know it's hard to improve on this favorite. But we just may have done so with this fun twist on tradition. We tested this recipe about a half a dozen times until we achieved the perfect consistency and flavor. To add the nutty, earthy taste characteristic of falafel, we use chickpea flour along with wheat flour in the batter. Chickpea flour is a wonderful plant-based protein that is high in fiber and a good source of iron! But don't worry about these being too dense: to help make the waffles airier, we use self-rising flour (see headnote on page 263) and add seltzer water instead of regular water (see notes on the next page).

We love to serve these savory waffles for brunch, topped with Spicy Israeli Salsa (page 62) and lots of Basic Tahini Sauce (page 133).

Prep time: 5 minutes
Cook time: 15 minutes
Makes 6 waffles

INGREDIENTS:

¾ cup self-rising flour

½ cup chickpea flour

1 tablespoon baking powder

2 teaspoons ground coriander

2 teaspoons ground cumin

2 teaspoons ground turmeric

1 teaspoon smoked paprika

1 teaspoon ground allspice

1 teaspoon garlic powder

½ teaspoon freshly ground
   black pepper

¼ teaspoon salt

1 cup seltzer water

3 tablespoons extra-virgin
   olive oil

Cooking spray or olive oil,
   for waffle iron

EQUIPMENT:

Waffle iron

Preheat your waffle iron according to the manufacturer's instructions.

In a large bowl, combine the self-rising and chickpea flours, baking powder, coriander, cumin, turmeric, smoked paprika, allspice, garlic powder, pepper, and salt and mix well. Add the seltzer water and olive oil and mix until all the ingredients are just incorporated.

Coat the waffle iron generously with cooking spray or olive oil. Spread with ⅓ cup of batter per waffle, close the iron, and let the waffle cook for 3 to 4 minutes, or until it releases easily from the iron. Repeat the process with the remaining batter, making sure to grease the iron before cooking each batch.

Serve warm.

notes: If you don't have seltzer water on hand, increase the amount of baking powder by ½ teaspoon.

Be sure to generously grease the waffle iron with cooking spray or olive oil, even if it has a nonstick surface.

mini spinach pies with pine nuts and dried cherries

If, like us, you entertain often, you are going to love this recipe. It's easy, it's bite-size (something people absolutely love), and it's a unique addition to any brunch menu. Almost like a vegan makeover on the traditional spinach quiche, with an unexpected sweet and tart touch from the cherries . . . only faster to prepare and a bit healthier! Vegan puff pastry is easily found in the freezer section of most grocery stores. Just thaw the pastry in the refrigerator before using, and keep it cold until you are ready to work with it. This will keep it from getting too soft and sticky.

Prep time: 5 minutes
Cook time: 35 minutes
Makes 24 pies

INGREDIENTS:

2 tablespoons extra-virgin olive oil

½ large sweet onion, diced (about 1 cup)

2 tablespoons pine nuts

¼ cup dried Bing cherries

16 ounces frozen spinach, thawed

½ teaspoon ground allspice

¼ teaspoon salt

2 vegan puff pastry sheets, thawed

All-purpose flour, for dusting

12 grape tomatoes, sliced in half

EQUIPMENT:

Parchment paper

Heat the olive oil in a large, nonstick skillet. Add the onion and cook over medium heat for 5 to 6 minutes, or until translucent.

Add the pine nuts to the skillet and cook for 2 minutes. Add the dried cherries and continue to cook for 4 more minutes, or until they start to soften.

Squeeze the water from the thawed spinach and add the spinach to the skillet, along with the allspice and salt. Continue to cook for 7 minutes, or until all the water has evaporated. Remove from the heat and set aside.

Preheat the oven to 400°F. Line a large baking sheet with parchment paper.

Place one sheet of puff pastry on a lightly floured surface (leave the other sheet in the refrigerator in the meantime) and stretch it out slightly with a rolling pin. Cut out twelve 2½-inch-diameter rounds and arrange them on the lined baking sheet.

> **TIME-SAVING TIP**
>
> Prepare the spinach up to three days in advance, and keep it refrigerated until you're ready to use it.

Spoon about 1 tablespoon of the spinach mixture onto each round, lightly pushing it down, and top each with a tomato half. Repeat the process with the other sheet of puff pastry. Bake for 20 minutes, or until golden brown. Serve immediately.

cashew ricotta stuffed syrian pancakes with orange blossom syrup (*atayef*)

Atayef are pancakes of Syrian origin that are traditionally stuffed with sweet ricotta-like cheese or ground nuts, and deep-fried. The batter is made with active yeast and cooked only on one side. The directions may seem a little complicated but don't worry—it's pretty easy! Our version is stuffed with homemade cashew "ricotta," panfried, and topped with orange blossom syrup and fresh pomegranate seeds for a touch of freshness.

Prep time: 45 minutes
Cook time: 45 minutes
Makes 28 pancakes

INGREDIENTS:

PANCAKE BATTER:

1¼ cups unsweetened
   almond milk

½ cup all-purpose flour

½ cup semolina flour

2 tablespoons sugar

½ teaspoon baking powder

½ teaspoon active dry yeast

1 teaspoon orange blossom water

½ cup plus 2 tablespoons
   neutral-flavor oil (such as
   grapeseed or avocado)

FILLING:

1 cup raw cashews

2 cups boiling water

⅓ cup sugar

1 teaspoon orange blossom water

ORANGE BLOSSOM SYRUP:

½ cup sugar

1½ teaspoons freshly squeezed
   lemon juice

1 teaspoon orange blossom water

GARNISH:

½ cup pomegranate seeds

¼ cup chopped pistachios

Combine all the batter ingredients, except the oil, in a blender and blend until smooth. Refrigerate for 30 minutes. At the same time, place the cashews for the filling in a bowl and cover with the boiling water; let them soak for 30 minutes.

In the meantime, prepare the orange blossom syrup: Combine the sugar and ¼ cup of water in a small saucepan and cook over medium heat for 2 to 3 minutes, or until the sugar has dissolved completely. Add the lemon juice and orange blossom water, lower the heat, and simmer for 5 minutes. Set aside until you are ready to use it.

TIME-SAVING TIP

You can prepare the orange blossom syrup ahead of time, and store it in the refrigerator for up to a month. The stuffed pancakes (before they are panfried) can also be made ahead of time and stored in the refrigerator, in an airtight container, for up to three days. Just bring them to room temperature and fry.

Prepare the filling: Drain the cashews (discarding the soak water) and place the cashews, sugar, and orange blossom water in a food processor. Pulse until the mixture is well combined and has a ricotta-like consistency (like a small curd).

To cook the pancakes, place 2 tablespoons of the oil in a small bowl. Heat a nonstick skillet over medium heat and brush it with some of the oil. Pour 1 tablespoon of batter onto the skillet, forming a circle about 3 inches in diameter. Cook on one side only for a little over a minute, or until bubbles start to form and the surface is no longer wet (if it is, cook for a few more seconds). Transfer the pancake to a plate, cooked side down (as you continue, make sure not to stack them, or else they will stick together). Repeat the process with the remaining batter, making sure to grease the skillet each time.

Once the pancakes are cool enough to handle, place 1 teaspoon of filling in the middle of the uncooked side of each one, fold it in half, and firmly press the end to seal the filled pancake in a shape of a half-moon.

Heat the remaining ½ cup of the oil in the same skillet. Fry the stuffed pancakes over medium-high heat, 1½ minutes per side, or until golden brown.

Serve warm, topped with orange blossom syrup, pomegranate seeds, and chopped pistachios.

nutty cinnamon rolls with halvah icing

These rolls are an easier, better-for-you version of the traditional breakfast treat. Even though they are still calorie dense, most of the sweetness of these rolls comes from dried apricots and dates, rather than added sugar; and the fat comes mainly from almonds and pistachios, rather than butter. If you're not familiar with halvah, be prepared to fall in love. It is a sweet made from tahini and sugar or honey, and it can definitely be addictive! The fragrant halvah icing adds a distinctive Middle Eastern touch. We like to make these rolls on weekends for breakfast or brunch, and they are a great way to indulge responsibly! We like using Trader Joe's or Immaculate Baking Company brand for our crescent roll dough.

Prep time: 15 minutes
Cook time: 35 minutes
Makes 12 rolls

INGREDIENTS:

Cooking spray, for pan

1½ cups dried apricots, roughly chopped

1 cup canned pure pumpkin puree

10 Medjool dates, pitted and roughly chopped

½ cup shelled roasted pistachios, plus 2 tablespoons for garnish

½ cup raw almonds

1½ tablespoons pure maple syrup

1½ tablespoons unsweetened nondairy milk

1 teaspoon ground cinnamon

2 (8-ounce) tubes vegan crescent roll dough

All-purpose flour, for dusting

HALVAH ICING:

3 tablespoons tahini

2 tablespoons pure maple syrup

1 tablespoon confectioners' sugar

⅛ teaspoon ground cardamom

2 tablespoons unsweetened nondairy milk

EQUIPMENT:

12-well jumbo or regular-size muffin tin

Preheat the oven to 350°F. Generously spray the bottom and sides of a twelve-well jumbo muffin tin with cooking spray (you can also use a regular-size muffin tin).

Combine the apricots, pumpkin, dates, ½ cup of pistachios, and the almonds, maple syrup, milk, and cinnamon in a food processor. Pulse until all the ingredients are well incorporated.

Place a large piece of waxed or parchment paper on the counter and flour it lightly. Unroll one tube of crescent roll dough over the floured paper, and roll it slightly with a rolling pin, just enough to seal the seams (leave the other tube in the refrigerator in the meantime).

Spread half of the filling over the dough, leaving about a ½-inch border on the longer sides.

Starting from the longer side closest to you, carefully roll up the dough while pressing it lightly (you can use the paper to help you). You will end up with a roll about 12 inches long. Using a serrated knife, cut the roll into six 2-inch lengths. Transfer the rolls, cut side up, to the prepared muffin tin.

TIME-SAVING TIP

The rolls can be prepared up to three days in advance and stored in the refrigerator, covered with plastic wrap. Let them sit at room temperature for 15 minutes before baking. You can also freeze the rolls after they are baked for up to a month.

Repeat the process with the other tube of dough. Bake for 30 to 32 minutes, or until golden brown.

A few minutes before the rolls are done, you can start to prepare the halvah icing. Whisk together all the icing ingredients, except the milk, in a medium-size bowl until well combined. Slowly pour in the milk, whisking constantly, until smooth and creamy.

Remove the rolls from the oven, let them cool slightly in the pan, and spoon the icing over them. Top with the reserved chopped pistachios and serve warm.

BELUGA LENTIL
BABA GHANOUSH

3

appetite teasers

Have you ever been to a restaurant where the appetizers were way better than the main courses? The kind of appetizers you'd be happy to eat as a meal? When we were growing up, every Friday night Mami spoiled us with an incredible spread of delicious meal starters, such as bulgur wheat patties, hummus, baba ghanoush, and kibbeh. As adults, whenever our sister Rebeca and her Israeli husband cooked for us, each dish they made was unbelievably fresh, hearty, and mouthwatering. They were especially skilled at tasty little salads, and their fried eggplant, pepper, and pickle chutney was our absolute favorite.

We have continued the tradition with our own families, making these dips, spreads, finger foods, and cooked vegetable salads to share. All these appetizers can be prepared ahead of time, and the leftovers make a great light lunch the next day.

Some call them meze, others call them tapas; we call them appetite teasers. These little plates to pass around and share make for a great bonding experience—and a fun and creative way to enjoy traditional Middle Eastern flavors with a modern twist.

creamy hummus with pine nuts and sumac

Warm hummus, made from dried chickpeas, is a real delicacy that is absolutely worth the extra time it takes to prepare. The chickpeas are soaked overnight in water and baking soda, so they cook faster (a trick we learned from our mom).

The hummus will thicken slightly once it's refrigerated. You can thin it out by adding one to two tablespoons of water and mixing well. Refrigerate for up to four days.

Prep time: 10 minutes (does not include overnight soaking time)
Cook time: 45 minutes
Makes 3 cups

INGREDIENTS:

1 cup dried chickpeas, soaked overnight in 4 cups water plus 1 teaspoon baking soda, plus more for garnish

1¼ teaspoons salt

2 teaspoons extra-virgin olive oil

2 tablespoons pine nuts

½ cup tahini

¼ cup freshly squeezed lemon juice, plus 1 to 2 tablespoons to taste

½ teaspoon sumac

Drain and rinse the soaked chickpeas. Combine them with 6 cups of water in a large saucepan. Bring the water to a boil, lower the heat to low, and simmer, uncovered, for 20 minutes. Using a slotted spoon, skim the white foam from the top. Add ½ teaspoon of the salt and continue to cook, uncovered, for an additional 20 to 25 minutes, or until the chickpeas are tender.

While the chickpeas are cooking, heat 1 teaspoon of the olive oil in a small skillet. Add the pine nuts and toast them for 1 to 2 minutes, stirring constantly, or until golden brown. Remove from the heat and set aside.

Combine the cooked chickpeas, tahini, lemon juice, 2 tablespoons of water, and the remaining ¾ teaspoon of salt in a food processor and process until smooth. Keep adding water, 1 tablespoon at a time, until you reach the desired consistency (you should use 4 to 6 tablespoons total). Serve warm or refrigerate until ready to serve.

Before serving, drizzle the hummus with the remaining teaspoon of olive oil, top with the toasted pine nuts and reserved chickpeas, and sprinkle with the sumac.

five-minute hummus

This quick version of the traditional hummus is perfect for when you are short on time, and it is still delicious! You can jazz it up by adding toppings, such as sumac, toasted pine nuts, chopped olives, sautéed onions, cooked mushrooms, or harissa paste, for a spicy kick. Served with fresh pita bread, crackers, or veggies, it's a great appetizer or on-the-go snack! Store in an airtight container in the refrigerator for up to four days.

Prep time: 5 minutes
Makes 2 cups

INGREDIENTS:

1 (15-ounce) can chickpeas, drained
  and rinsed

½ cup tahini

¼ teaspoon salt

⅓ cup freshly squeezed lemon juice

1 garlic clove (optional)

Extra-virgin olive oil, for garnish

Combine all the ingredients, except the olive oil, in a food processor and add ¼ cup of water. Process until smooth and creamy. Drizzle with extra-virgin olive oil before serving.

deconstructed hummus

The name of this dish in Arabic is *msabaha*, which translates to "swimming," because the chickpeas are "swimming" in tahini sauce. We call this recipe "deconstructed hummus" because it is basically a combination of all the hummus ingredients, but presented separately instead of blended together. Just like the dip, it's served as part of the selection of meze, and scooped right out of the bowl with fresh pita bread.

Prep time: 10 minutes
Cook time: 45 minutes
Makes 4 servings

INGREDIENTS:

1 cup dried chickpeas, soaked
  overnight in 4 cups water plus 1
  teaspoon baking soda, or 2¾ cups
  canned, drained and rinsed

½ teaspoon salt

1 teaspoon extra-virgin olive oil

2 tablespoons pine nuts

Basic Tahini Sauce (page 133)

½ cup chopped fresh parsley

½ teaspoon sweet paprika

Drain and rinse the soaked chickpeas. Combine them with 6 cups of water in a large saucepan. Bring the water to a boil, lower the heat to low, and simmer, uncovered, for 20 minutes. Using a slotted spoon, skim the white foam from the top. Add the salt and continue to cook, uncovered, for an additional 20 to 25 minutes, or until the chickpeas are tender. (Skip this step if using canned chickpeas.)

Heat the olive oil in a small skillet. Add the pine nuts and toast them over medium heat for 1 to 2 minutes, stirring constantly, or until golden brown. Remove from the heat and set aside.

If using canned chickpeas, rinse and drain them, and heat them in a small saucepan over medium heat for 2 to 3 minutes.

Serve the chickpeas warm, topped with tahini sauce, the toasted pine nuts, and the parsley and sweet paprika.

tangy roasted carrot hummus

Roasted carrots add a wonderful, natural sweetness to this hummus. Combined with creamy chickpeas, tahini, lots of fresh lemon juice, and a sprinkle of *dukkah* (page 130), this recipe is a great balance of sweet and savory, reminiscent of the traditional Moroccan carrot salad. Even though this calls for ½ cup of lemon juice, which may seem like a lot, it needs the acidity to balance the sweetness of the carrots.

Serve with pita chips or crackers, or instead of mayonnaise on sandwiches or wraps.

Store the hummus in an airtight container in the refrigerator for up to five days. It will thicken slightly when refrigerated.

Prep time: 10 minutes
Cook time: 55 minutes
Makes 3½ cups

INGREDIENTS:

1 cup dried chickpeas, soaked overnight in 4 cups water plus 1 teaspoon baking soda, or 2¾ cups canned, drained and rinsed

1 teaspoon salt

3 medium-size carrots, peeled and trimmed

1 tablespoon extra-virgin olive oil, plus more for drizzling

½ cup tahini

½ cup freshly squeezed lemon juice

2 to 4 tablespoons Dukkah (page 130)

EQUIPMENT:
Parchment paper

Drain and rinse the soaked chickpeas. Combine them with 6 cups of water in a large saucepan. Bring the water to a boil, lower the heat to low, and simmer, uncovered, for 20 minutes. Using a slotted spoon, skim the white foam from the top. Add ½ teaspoon of the salt and continue to cook, uncovered, for an additional 20 to 25 minutes, or until the chickpeas are tender.

While the chickpeas cook, preheat the oven to 375°F. Line a baking sheet with parchment paper.

Place the carrots in a bowl. Drizzle them with the tablespoon of olive oil, making sure the oil coats all sides of the carrots. Transfer them to the lined baking sheet and bake for 40 minutes. Remove from the oven and set aside.

Once the chickpeas are ready, drain them, reserving about ½ cup of the cooking water (if you forget to reserve the cooking water, use regular water). Let cool slightly.

Combine the cooked chickpeas, roasted carrots, tahini, lemon juice, and remaining ½ teaspoon of salt in a food processor. Process until smooth. Add the reserved chickpea water, 1 tablespoon at a time, until you achieve the desired creamy consistency (you might not need the whole ½ cup you reserved).

Drizzle with olive oil and sprinkle with *dukkah* before serving.

whipped white bean and cilantro dip

There are two kinds of people in this world: those who love cilantro, and those who are absolutely not fond of it. We're Team Cilantro all the way, thanks to our dad, as you will see in many of our recipes, especially the ones inspired by him. We love its earthy, herby, almost sweet flavor and the stunning color it adds to our dishes. But we understand that not everyone feels the same way, so if that's the case, feel free to use fresh parsley instead.

This dip is great as an appetizer or on-the-go snack, served with crackers, tortilla chips, or vegetables. Store the dip in an airtight container in the refrigerator for up to four days.

Prep time: 10 minutes
Makes 1⅓ cups

INGREDIENTS:

1 (15-ounce) can cannellini beans, drained and rinsed

1 cup lightly packed fresh cilantro leaves

3 tablespoons freshly squeezed lemon juice

½ teaspoon ground cumin

½ teaspoon salt

2 tablespoons extra-virgin olive oil, plus a little more for drizzling

Za'atar, for garnish

Combine the beans, cilantro, lemon juice, cumin, and salt in a food processor. Pulse while drizzling in the olive oil, until smooth and creamy. Serve with a drizzle of extra-virgin olive oil and a sprinkle of za'atar.

velvety white bean and beet dip with pine nuts

We've always loved beets. When we moved to the United States and learned how many people are not very fond of them, we were truly shocked! We created this dip as a way to highlight their earthy, sweet flavor. Serve with crackers, pita chips, or cut-up veggies as an appetizer or light lunch—or even as a sandwich spread! Store it in the refrigerator for up to five days.

Prep time: 10 minutes
Cook time: 1 hour
Makes 2¼ cups

INGREDIENTS:

3 medium-size red beets, thoroughly washed

2 tablespoons plus 1 teaspoon extra-virgin olive oil

2 tablespoons raw pine nuts

1 (15-ounce) can cannellini beans, drained and rinsed

3 tablespoons freshly squeezed lemon juice

¾ teaspoon ground cumin

½ teaspoon salt

> TIME-SAVING TIP
> Use store-bought cooked beets, but take into consideration that the color of the dip will be a darker burgundy rather than vibrant pink.

Preheat the oven to 375°F. Wrap each beet in aluminum foil. Place on a baking sheet and bake for 1 hour, or until tender. Remove from the oven and let cool until safe to handle with your hands.

While the beets are cooking, heat 1 teaspoon of the olive oil in a small skillet, add the pine nuts, and toast for 1 to 2 minutes, stirring constantly, or until golden. Set aside.

Once the beets have cooled, remove the skin and cut the beets into quarters.

Combine the cut beets, beans, lemon juice, cumin, and salt in a food processor. Pulse until smooth. While the food processor is on, drizzle in the remaining 2 tablespoons of olive oil. Refrigerate until ready to use.

Serve with toasted pine nuts and a drizzle of olive oil.

warm citrusy fava beans with pita chips

This traditional Middle Eastern dish is one of the easiest and quickest appetizers or light dinners you'll ever make! It's warm, hearty, full of flavor, and best of all, extremely easy to prepare.

For this dish you will need canned fava beans, usually found only in Middle Eastern stores or online under the name *ful mudammas* (some natural grocery stores may carry them). We suggest you buy a few cans and store them in your pantry!

Store the prepared fava beans in the refrigerator for up to three days, and the pita chips in a resealable container in a dry, cool place for up to five days.

Prep time: 10 minutes
Cook time: 20 minutes
Makes 4 servings

INGREDIENTS:

2 pita breads, opened and separated along the edge into 4 disks

2 tablespoons extra-virgin olive oil

1 teaspoon sumac

1 teaspoon dried oregano

¼ teaspoon salt

FAVA BEANS:

20 ounces canned fava beans (*ful mudammas*), with their liquid

2 tablespoons freshly squeezed lemon juice, or to taste

2 garlic cloves, crushed

½ teaspoon salt

½ teaspoon ground cumin

1 tablespoon extra-virgin olive oil

2 tablespoons chopped fresh parsley

Preheat the oven to 375°F. Line a large baking sheet with aluminum foil.

Prepare the pita chips first: Drizzle about 1½ teaspoons of olive oil on each pita disk.

Combine the sumac, oregano, and salt in a small bowl and mix well. Sprinkle evenly over the pita disks, transfer them to the lined baking sheet, and bake for 5 to 7 minutes, or until crispy. Remove from the oven and let them cool slightly, then break them into pieces. Set aside.

Prepare the fava beans: Combine the fava beans, ½ cup of water, lemon juice, garlic, salt, and cumin in a small saucepan. Cook over medium heat for 10 to 15 minutes.

Serve the warm fava beans in a bowl, with a drizzle of olive oil, garnished with chopped parsley, and with the pita chips on the side.

fried eggplant, pepper, and pickle chutney

We learned this simple yet delicious recipe from our Israeli brother-in-law, who prepares it every Friday night as part of an appetizer spread. The zesty pickles balance the fried peppers and eggplant perfectly, and the spices give the chutney a great punch of flavor. Serve this with pita bread or crackers or, as our brother-in-law does, as part of a selection of meze or tapas.

Store in the refrigerator for up to five days.

Prep time: 30 minutes
Cook time: 20 minutes
Makes 3 cups

INGREDIENTS:

3 Japanese eggplants, unpeeled, diced (about 3 cups)

1¼ teaspoons salt

½ cup neutral-flavor oil (such as sunflower, grapeseed, or avocado)

2 red bell peppers, seeded and diced (about 2 cups)

5 Israeli-style pickles or 12 to 15 cornichons, chopped (about 1 cup)

¾ teaspoon sweet paprika

½ teaspoon ground cumin

½ teaspoon Aleppo pepper

1 tablespoon red wine vinegar

TIP

It's important to fry the peppers before frying the eggplant. Otherwise, the eggplant will absorb most of the oil and you will need to add more, making the chutney too oily and heavy.

Place the diced eggplant and 1 teaspoon of the salt in a colander with a bowl underneath to collect the liquid the eggplant will release. Let sit for 15 minutes.

Line a large plate with paper towels and place it near the stove. Heat the oil in a small saucepan. Add 1 cup of the diced red peppers and fry over medium heat for 5 minutes.

Using a slotted spoon, remove the peppers from the oil and transfer them to the lined plate, so the paper towels absorb the excess oil. Repeat the process with the remaining cup of red peppers.

Add the diced eggplant to the oil and fry for 10 minutes, or until tender.

Combine the fried peppers and eggplant in a large bowl. Add the chopped pickles, sweet paprika, cumin, Aleppo pepper, vinegar, and remaining ¼ teaspoon of salt. Toss well and refrigerate for 15 to 20 minutes, so the flavors start to blend together.

spicy tomato and pepper jam

This traditional dish is known as *matbuja* in Arabic, *salade cuite* in French (in Morocco), and *salat mevushal* in Hebrew. It's best when prepared during the summer months when the tomatoes are sweet and juicy. Freeze in small jars, so you can enjoy it throughout the year!

Serve with toasted crusty bread, pita chips, or crackers.

Prep time: 10 minutes
Cook time: 2 hours 45 minutes
Makes 4 to 5 cups

INGREDIENTS:

6 pounds tomatoes (about 12 large)

¼ cup extra-virgin olive oil

8 large garlic cloves, sliced

2 tablespoons sweet paprika

1½ teaspoons salt

5 to 6 jalapeño peppers, diced

Fill a large soup pot with water about halfway and bring to a boil over high heat.

Using a sharp knife, score the bottom of each tomato with an X. Carefully place them in the boiling water, using tongs or a large slotted spoon, and cook for 5 minutes.

Using a slotted spoon, remove the tomatoes from boiling water and let cool until safe to handle with your hands. Remove the skin and the stems and chop the flesh roughly.

TIP
You can also use canned whole tomatoes, and skip the tomato-peeling step. Adjust salt to 1 teaspoon unless using salt-free canned tomatoes.

Heat the olive oil in a large, deep skillet with a lid. Add the garlic, sweet paprika, and salt and cook for 2 minutes over medium heat, stirring frequently and watching it carefully so the garlic doesn't burn. Add the jalapeños and continue to cook for 5 minutes.

Add the chopped tomatoes, bring to a boil, lower the heat to low, and simmer, covered, for 2 to 2½ hours, or until the tomato mixture has reduced by half. Stir frequently throughout the cooking process. Remove from the heat, let cool completely, then store in the refrigerator in glass jars or an airtight container.

chunky eggplant, carrot, and walnut salsa

The inspiration for this recipe comes from a Syrian dish called *makdous*, a real delicacy that our parents made when we were kids, and still make today. Baby eggplants are boiled and stuffed with walnuts, carrots, and garlic, then tightly fitted into a jar and covered with olive oil. The jar is left at room temperature for about a week, which causes the eggplant to start fermenting lightly, creating a tangy bite.

This recipe re-creates the same flavors of the traditional *makdous*, but the preparation is far less time consuming. Serve the salsa with fresh pita bread or toasted baguette slices. Store in the refrigerator for up to three days.

Prep time: 1 hour 15 minutes
Cook time: 20 minutes
Makes 3 cups

INGREDIENTS:

2 teaspoons sweet paprika

1 teaspoon ground turmeric

½ teaspoon ground cumin

½ teaspoon salt

⅛ teaspoon freshly ground black pepper

2 Japanese eggplants, unpeeled, cut into ½-inch dice (about 5 cups)

3 tablespoons extra-virgin olive oil

12 kalamata olives, pitted and sliced in half

12 black cured olives, pitted and sliced in half

1 cup shredded carrot

⅓ cup walnut halves, chopped

¼ cup chopped fresh parsley

2 tablespoons red wine vinegar

1 garlic clove, grated (optional)

1 teaspoon chopped jarred marinated hot cherry peppers

EQUIPMENT:

Parchment paper

Preheat the oven to 400°F. Line a large baking sheet with parchment paper.

Combine the sweet paprika, turmeric, cumin, salt, and black pepper in a small bowl. Mix well and set aside.

Place the diced eggplant in a large bowl. Add 2 tablespoons of the olive oil and the spice mixture and toss well, so the eggplant is well coated with the spices. Transfer the eggplant to the prepared baking sheet and bake for 20 minutes, or until tender. Remove from the oven and let cool.

Combine the cooked eggplant, olives, carrot, walnuts, parsley, vinegar, garlic (if using), remaining tablespoon of olive oil, and hot cherry peppers in a large bowl and toss gently. Cover with plastic wrap and let sit in the refrigerator for 1 hour before serving.

spicy israeli salsa

This simple yet flavorful salad is our dad's Friday night staple. During the summer, he picks the tomatoes and cucumbers from his garden, and adds a generous amount of jalapeño peppers. If you don't like a lot of heat, feel free to use a smaller amount of peppers. Be aware, however, that not all jalapeños have the same heat level! Some are a lot hotter than others. Make sure to thoroughly wash your hands after cutting them, and remember never to touch your eyes (we've learned that lesson the hard way . . .).

It's better to enjoy this salad the same day it's prepared. Once it sits for too long, the tomatoes might become a little too soggy.

Prep time: 10 minutes
Makes 4 to 6 servings

INGREDIENTS:

1 pound assorted colored tomatoes, diced small

5 to 6 Persian cucumbers, diced small

2 to 3 jalapeño peppers, diced small

½ cup chopped fresh cilantro

2 tablespoons extra-virgin olive oil

2 tablespoons freshly squeezed lemon juice

¼ to ½ teaspoon salt

Combine all the ingredients in a large bowl and toss well. Refrigerate until you are ready to serve.

beluga lentil and baba ghanoush toast

When we were kids, tahini was difficult to find in Spain. To us it was an uncommon treat, and we only got to enjoy some of our favorite Middle Eastern staples, such as hummus or baba ghanoush, on special occasions. Thankfully, tahini is available abundantly in the United States. We have transformed this classic Middle Eastern dip into a complete meal by adding hearty beluga lentils for protein and pomegranate seeds for sweetness and crunch. We love it slathered on toasted country bread, but it also works great as a dip, served with fresh pita bread wedges.

Prep time: 45 minutes
Cook time: 1 hour
Makes 4 to 6 servings

INGREDIENTS:

2 large eggplants

1 teaspoon salt

½ cup dried black beluga lentils, picked over and rinsed

¼ cup plus 1 tablespoon tahini

⅓ cup freshly squeezed lemon juice (from about 1½ large lemons)

2 tablespoons black sesame seeds

1 cup pomegranate seeds (from about 1 medium-size pomegranate)

¾ cup chopped fresh parsley

1 loaf crusty vegan whole-grain country bread or Za'atar and Seed Bread (page 225), sliced and toasted

Preheat the oven to BROIL. Line a large baking sheet with aluminum foil or parchment paper.

Poke the eggplants on all sides with a knife twenty to thirty times (depending on their size), and place on the lined baking sheet. Broil for 30 minutes on each side.

TIME-SAVING TIP

The eggplant can be broiled two to three days ahead of time. Scoop out the flesh and store it in the refrigerator, in an airtight container. Discard any excess liquid before making the baba ghanoush.

Remove the eggplants from the oven and let sit until they're cool enough to handle, about 20 minutes.

In the meantime, combine 6 cups of water and ½ teaspoon of the salt in a large saucepan. Bring to a boil over high heat. Add the rinsed lentils and cook, uncovered, over medium heat for 20 to 25 minutes, or until tender but slightly firm. Drain well.

Cut the eggplants in half, and with the help of a spoon, scoop out all the flesh, discarding the skin and as many seeds as possible (you should end up with about 1½ cups of eggplant). Transfer the flesh to a colander with a bowl underneath, and let sit for 20 minutes. Discard any drained liquid.

Place the eggplant in a large glass bowl and mash it with a fork. Add the tahini, lemon juice, and ½ teaspoon of the salt and mix until well incorporated.

Right before serving, add the sesame seeds, pomegranate seeds, cooked lentils, and parsley and mix gently. Serve over the toasted bread. Store any remaining spread in the refrigerator for up to four days.

stuffed avocados

We absolutely love the combination of avocado and chickpeas. Not only is it delicious, but a nutritional powerhouse, too!

Choose avocados that are slightly firm to the touch. Make sure to slice and stuff them right before serving, to keep them from turning brown.

Prep time: 5 minutes
Cook time: 10 minutes
Makes 4 servings

INGREDIENTS:

2 teaspoons smoked paprika

½ teaspoon ground cumin

½ teaspoon ground turmeric

½ teaspoon salt

⅛ teaspoon freshly ground black pepper

1 (15-ounce) can chickpeas, drained and rinsed

1 tablespoon extra-virgin olive oil

10 fresh mint leaves, chopped

2 tablespoons freshly squeezed lemon juice (from about ½ lemon)

1 tablespoon za'atar

2 slightly firm Hass avocados

Combine the smoked paprika, cumin, turmeric, salt, and pepper in a small bowl. Add the drained chickpeas and toss well, so they are well coated with the spices.

> TIME-SAVING TIP
> You can prepare the chickpeas up to three days in advance and store them in an airtight container in the refrigerator.

Heat the olive oil in a large, nonstick skillet. Add the chickpeas and mix gently, so they are well coated with the oil. Cook over medium heat for 5 to 7 minutes. Transfer them to a bowl while they're warm; add the chopped mint, lemon juice, and za'atar; and toss well. Set aside.

Right before serving, slice the avocados in half. Remove the pit and spoon the chickpeas onto each half.

STUFFED AVOCADOS

CRISPY MINI MEATLESS PIES

crispy mini meatless pies

This delicious appetizer is one of our family's favorites. The inspiration comes from a dish called *lajme bil ajin* (which translates to "meat on the dough"), which our mom would often make on Friday nights or special occasions. The traditional version is made with homemade pizza dough, topped with ground beef sautéed in olive oil with pine nuts, chopped tomatoes, and pomegranate molasses. We have simplified the recipe by using crispy spring roll wrappers as a base, and substituted tofu for the ground meat.

If you would like to freeze these, arrange them on a large baking sheet before they're baked, and place in the freezer for about two hours (this will keep the filling from falling off). Transfer to a large freezer bag and freeze for up to a month.

Prep time: 15 minutes
Cook time: 35 minutes
Makes 18 pies

INGREDIENTS:

2 tablespoons plus ½ teaspoon extra-virgin olive oil

1 medium-size onion, diced (about 1 cup)

10 ounces extra-firm tofu, patted dry

½ cup chopped fresh parsley

3 tablespoons sun-dried tomatoes packed in oil, diced

¼ cup pomegranate molasses (see page 132 for homemade)

1 teaspoon salt

½ teaspoon ground cinnamon

½ teaspoon baharat or ground allspice

2 tablespoons raw pine nuts

9 spring roll wrappers

¼ cup vegetable oil

EQUIPMENT:

Parchment paper

Heat 1 tablespoon of the olive oil in a large, nonstick pan. Add the diced onion and cook over medium heat for 10 minutes, until translucent.

Crumble the tofu into a medium-size bowl. Add the cooked onion, parsley, diced sun-dried tomatoes, pomegranate molasses, salt, cinnamon, and baharat and mix well.

Using the same pan, heat 1 tablespoon of olive oil. Add the tofu mixture and cook over medium-high heat for 10 minutes, stirring occasionally. Transfer to a bowl and set aside.

In the same skillet, heat the remaining ½ teaspoon of olive oil. Add the pine nuts and toast for 1 to 2 minutes, stirring frequently and watching carefully to prevent them from burning. Remove from the heat and set aside.

Preheat the oven to 375°F. Line two baking sheets with parchment paper.

Brush each spring roll wrapper on both sides with vegetable oil. Cut each wrapper in half and fold each half into a square (you will end up with 18 squares).

Spoon a heaping tablespoon of tofu mixture into the middle of each wrapper square, lightly pushing it down so it almost covers the surface of the wrapper. Sprinkle the toasted pine nuts on top and transfer to the lined baking sheets (9 per sheet). Bake for 12 to 15 minutes, or until golden brown.

TIP

To make sure the wrappers don't dry out while you fold them, pile them on top of one another and cover with a clean towel until they are ready to be filled and baked.

bulgur wheat patties with spicy tahini dipping sauce

This recipe is, in our opinion, one of the cleverest uses of leftovers we've seen. Our mom makes kibbeh very often (see page 199), and uses the leftover dough to make these delicious patties. She normally fries them, which makes them really crispy, and serves them with tahini sauce. To lighten them up a little bit, we bake ours instead, and for a touch of heat, we add some hot sauce to the traditional tahini sauce.

The baked patties can be stored in the refrigerator for up to four days, or in the freezer for up to a month.

Prep time: 30 minutes
Cook time: 20 minutes
Makes 20 patties

INGREDIENTS:

1 cup fine (#1) bulgur wheat

1 cup boiling water

1 cup canned pure pumpkin puree

⅓ cup all-purpose flour

3 tablespoons extra-virgin olive oil

2 teaspoons sweet paprika

1 teaspoon salt

½ teaspoon ground cumin

½ teaspoon ground turmeric

SPICY TAHINI SAUCE:

½ cup tahini

¼ cup freshly squeezed lemon juice,
   plus 2 tablespoons (optional)

½ teaspoon salt

Hot sauce or sriracha

EQUIPMENT:

Parchment paper

Preheat the oven to 375°F. Line a large baking sheet with parchment paper.

Place the bulgur wheat and boiling water in a large, heatproof bowl. Cover with a large plate and let sit for 20 minutes, or until all the water has been absorbed. Squeeze out any excess water with your hands.

Add the pumpkin, flour, olive oil, sweet paprika, salt, cumin, and turmeric to the bulgur. Mix well, using your hands, until it comes together to form a dough.

Working with 1½ tablespoons of mixture at a time, form balls of dough. Lightly flatten each ball with the palm of your hand to make a 2-inch-diameter patty.

Arrange the patties on the lined baking sheet and bake for 20 minutes.

To prepare the spicy tahini sauce, whisk together the tahini, lemon juice, and salt in a small bowl until thickened. Add 1 tablespoon of water at a time, whisking constantly until creamy (use up to ¼ cup total). Taste and add more lemon juice if needed. Add the hot sauce and mix well.

Serve the patties warm with the spicy tahini sauce on the side.

TIP

If you don't have canned pumpkin handy, you can use a cup of mashed potatoes instead (about 2 medium-size potatoes, boiled and mashed) and add an extra ¼ cup of water.

bulgur wheat tartare

The Lebanese version of steak tartare is called *kibbeh nayeh* (which means "raw kibbe"), which combines raw bulgur wheat, green onions, and olive oil. Our version omits the meat and incorporates bell peppers, parsley, and a touch of pomegranate molasses. The sliced beet gives the bulgur a meatlike, pinkish color. This step can be skipped without at all affecting the taste of the dish.

Store the tartare in the refrigerator for up to three days. It can also be prepared a day ahead of time.

Prep time: 30 minutes
Makes 4 servings

INGREDIENTS:

1 cup fine (#1) bulgur wheat

1 small red beet, peeled and sliced

1 cup boiling water

1 small red bell pepper, seeded and diced small

1 small green bell pepper, seeded and diced small

3 scallions, thinly sliced

½ cup tightly packed fresh parsley, chopped

3 tablespoons pomegranate molasses

2 tablespoons freshly squeezed lemon juice

1 tablespoon extra-virgin olive oil

1 teaspoon salt

½ teaspoon freshly ground black pepper

½ teaspoon baharat or ground allspice

Place the bulgur wheat in a medium-size heatproof bowl. Bury the beet slices inside, pour the boiling water over the bulgur wheat, cover with a plate, and let sit for 20 minutes, or until all the water has been absorbed. Squeeze out any excess water with your hands.

Remove the beets and mix well, so the color distributes evenly.

Transfer the wheat to a large bowl. Add the peppers, scallions, and parsley and toss well. Add the remaining ingredients and mix well. Refrigerate until you're ready to serve.

ombre roasted beet salad
with cumin dressing

Our friends often ask why we roast beets instead of boiling them, which saves some time. And yes, roasting might take a little longer. However, it brings out their natural sweetness and preserves their beautiful, vibrant color.

You can prepare this dish using as many different color beets as you can find, for a stunning, colorful presentation. Don't forget to separate them by color before serving, to prevent them from bleeding.

Prep time: 10 minutes
Cook time: 1 hour
Makes 4 to 6 servings

INGREDIENTS:

2 medium-size white beets, thoroughly washed

2 medium-size orange or yellow beets, thoroughly washed

2 medium-size pink beets, thoroughly washed

2 medium-size red beets, thoroughly washed

1 cup chopped fresh cilantro

Cumin Dressing (page 135)

¼ cup chopped walnuts

Preheat the oven to 375°F. Wrap each beet in aluminum foil. Place on a baking sheet and bake for 1 hour, or until tender. Remove from the oven and let cool until safe to handle with your hands.

Once the beets have cooled, remove the skin and dice each beet separately. Transfer to four separate bowls, according to color.

Add ¼ cup of the chopped cilantro to each bowl and mix well.

Before serving, arrange the beets from light to dark on a serving platter. Drizzle with the cumin dressing and top with the walnuts.

> **TIME-SAVING TIP**
>
> The roasted beets can be prepared ahead of time and stored in the refrigerator for up to three days.

roasted beets, avocado, and persimmons with sumac tahini

The most commonly found persimmons in the United States are Fuyu and the Israeli varieties called Sharon and Hachiya. Hachiya persimmons are shaped like a large acorn, and it's best to eat them when they are very soft and ripe. Otherwise, they will leave a very unpleasant, cottony feel in your mouth. Fuyu and Sharon persimmons, on the other hand, can be eaten firm. They're always sweet, and there is no need to worry about their texture, which is why we use them for this recipe. It pairs beautifully with the Crispy Mini Meatless Pies (page 70).

Prep time: 10 minutes
Cook time: 1 hour
Makes 4 servings

INGREDIENTS:

2 medium-size red beets

1 teaspoon sumac

Basic Tahini Sauce (see page 133)

2 Fuyu or Sharon persimmons, peeled, seeded, and sliced

½ Hass avocado, peeled, pitted, and sliced

¼ cup chopped fresh cilantro

Preheat the oven to 375°F. Wrap each beet in aluminum foil. Place on a baking sheet and bake for 1 hour, or until tender when pierced with a fork. Remove from the oven and let cool until safe to handle with your hands.

Once the beets have cooled, remove the skin and slice the beets.

To prepare the sumac tahini, add the sumac to the prepared tahini sauce and mix well.

Before serving, arrange the sliced persimmons, beets, and avocado on a serving platter. Drizzle with the sumac tahini and garnish with the chopped cilantro.

> TIME-SAVING TIP
>
> The roasted beets can be prepared ahead of time, and stored in the refrigerator for up to three days. You can also use store-bought, precooked beets, which can be found in the refrigerated produce section of most grocery stores.

roasted eggplant coins with silan, pomegranates, and pistachios

The combination of silan and tahini is pretty much the Middle Eastern equivalent of peanut butter and jelly. Our parents love to mix them in a bowl and use as a dip for pita bread, as a dessert or snack. We love to add it to savory dishes, such as this appetizer. The sweet silan and nutty tahini combined with the creamy eggplant is absolutely out of this world. The crunchy pistachios and pomegranate seeds add a great texture to the dish.

Prep time: 10 minutes
Cook time: 30 minutes
Makes 4 to 6 servings

INGREDIENTS:

3 tablespoons extra-virgin olive oil

4 Japanese eggplants sliced unpeeled, into ½-inch-thick slices

¼ teaspoon salt

2 tablespoons tahini

1 tablespoon silan

¼ cup pomegranate seeds

¼ cup chopped pistachios

EQUIPMENT:

Parchment paper

Preheat the oven to 375°F. Line a large baking sheet with parchment paper. Brush the paper with 1 tablespoon of the olive oil.

TIME-SAVING TIP

The eggplant can be roasted up to three days in advance, and kept refrigerated until ready to use.

Arrange the eggplant slices on the lined baking sheet. Drizzle the remaining 2 tablespoons of olive oil on top and sprinkle with the salt. Bake for 30 minutes, or until tender.

Right before serving, arrange the eggplant slices on a platter, drizzle with the tahini and silan, and top with the pomegranate seeds and pistachios.

HEARTY SPICED CHICKPEAS,
LENTIL, AND ROOT VEGETABLE SOUP

4

body warmers

Growing up in Barcelona where winters are pretty mild, we didn't eat soup very often. But when we did, it was always homemade. We didn't know what real cold weather was until we moved to the East Coast of the United States twenty years ago. Now, soup is a cherished comfort food in our homes. Inspired by our mom's homemade soups, these recipes are full of warming and healing spices, such as paprika, turmeric, and cumin. Hearty and easy to prepare, they'll make you forget about that stuff you get in a can. Oh, and they are incredibly nutritious, too! We use beans, from lentils to chickpeas, for protein; they are also high in fiber and very filling. Most of these soups make an excellent light lunch.

veggie soup for the soul

This soup is the one our mom made most frequently when we were kids, especially when one of us was feeling under the weather. Full of chunky vegetables in a spiced tomato broth, it is comforting and incredibly satisfying.

This recipe yields a large amount of soup; it can be frozen for up to two months.

Prep time: 20 minutes
Cook time: 1 hour
Makes 5½ quarts

INGREDIENTS:

2 tablespoons extra-virgin olive oil

1½ tablespoons smoked paprika

1 tablespoon ground turmeric

1½ teaspoons onion powder

1½ teaspoons garlic powder

6 ounces tomato paste

8 cups vegetable or no-chicken vegetarian broth

1½ pounds butternut squash, peeled, seeded, and cut into large dice

3 large carrots, peeled and sliced into ½-inch slices

2 leeks, thoroughly washed and cut into ½-inch pieces

2 large green zucchini, thoroughly washed and cut into large dice

1 large rutabaga, peeled and cut into large dice

1 large parsnip, peeled and cut into large dice

1 large turnip, peeled and cut into large dice

2½ teaspoons salt, or to taste

¼ teaspoon freshly ground black pepper

Heat the olive oil in a large soup pot. Add the smoked paprika, turmeric, onion, and garlic powder and cook over medium-low heat for 30 seconds, stirring constantly. Add the tomato paste and continue to cook for 1 minute, stirring constantly.

Add 8 cups water, the broth, all the vegetables, and the salt and pepper and increase the heat to medium-high heat. Cook until the mixture comes to a boil, about 18 minutes.

Lower the heat to low and simmer, partially covered, for 40 minutes, or until the vegetables are tender.

hearty spiced chickpea, lentil, and root vegetable soup

The inspiration for this recipe comes from a traditional Moroccan soup called *harira*. Full of vegetables, beans, and spices, it's incredibly satisfying and bursting with flavor. Serve it with a chunk of Za'atar and Seed Bread (page 225) and Spiced Toasted Bulgur Salad with Tahini Dressing (page 123) for a hearty lunch or light dinner. Store in the refrigerator for up to four days, or in the freezer for up to a month.

Prep time: 20 minutes
Cook time: 1 hour
Makes 3 quarts

INGREDIENTS:

2 teaspoons salt

1½ teaspoons ground turmeric

1 teaspoon ground cumin

¼ teaspoon freshly ground black pepper

2 tablespoons extra-virgin olive oil

1 medium-size onion, diced (about 1 cup)

3 garlic cloves, minced

2 large carrots, diced

2 parsnips, diced

1 medium-size celery root, diced

1 small rutabaga, diced

½ cup dried red lentils, picked over and rinsed well

½ cup dried French lentils, picked over and rinsed well

1 (15-ounce) can chickpeas

1 (28-ounce) can diced tomatoes

1 cup chopped fresh cilantro

Combine the salt, turmeric, cumin, and pepper in a small bowl and set aside.

Heat the olive oil in a large soup pot. Add the onion and garlic and cook over medium heat for 8 to 10 minutes, stirring frequently, or until the onion starts to brown slightly.

Add the spice mixture to the pot and cook for 2 to 3 minutes, stirring frequently.

Add the carrots, parsnips, celery root, and rutabaga and continue to cook for 3 to 5 minutes.

Add 6 cups of water, the red and French lentils, and the chickpeas. Bring the soup to a boil, lower the heat, then simmer, covered, for 30 minutes, or until the lentils and vegetables are tender.

Add the canned tomatoes, bring to a boil, lower the heat, and simmer, covered, for an additional 15 to 20 minutes.

Remove from the heat, add the cilantro, and stir well.

meal-in-a-bowl bean and israeli couscous soup

Inspired by our mom's vegetable soup (Veggie Soup for the Soul, page 86), we created our own hearty version by adding chickpeas, black beans, and Israeli couscous. It's substantial enough to serve as a meal on its own. Store in the refrigerator for up to five days, or in the freezer for up to a month.

Prep time: 15 minutes
Cook time: 55 minutes
Makes 3 quarts

INGREDIENTS:

2 tablespoons extra-virgin olive oil

2 tablespoons tomato paste

½ teaspoon salt

¼ teaspoon freshly ground black pepper

3 medium-size carrots, sliced

1 medium-size onion, diced

3 celery stalks, sliced

1 small shallot, diced

2 tablespoons Good-on-Everything Spice Mix (page 131)

2 tablespoons (or 2 cubes) vegetable bouillon

1 (28-ounce) can diced tomatoes

1 (15-ounce) can black beans, drained and rinsed

1 (15-ounce) can chickpeas, drained and rinsed

2 medium-size zucchini, diced

⅓ cup Israeli couscous

½ cup chopped fresh parsley or cilantro

Heat the olive oil in a large stockpot. Add the tomato paste, salt, and pepper, and cook over medium heat for 2 minutes, stirring constantly. Add the carrots, onion, celery, and shallot, and cook for 10 minutes. Add the spice mix and continue to cook for 2 to 3 minutes.

Add 6 cups of water, the vegetable bouillon, and the diced tomatoes, black beans, and chickpeas. Bring to a boil, lower the heat, and simmer for 20 minutes. Add the zucchini and Israeli couscous, stir well, and simmer for an additional 20 minutes.

Turn off the heat and add the parsley or cilantro before serving.

saffron-infused cauliflower soup with sumac oil

After our move to the United States, freezing winters (at least compared to our winters in Barcelona) and endless snowy days called for a hot, steamy bowl of soup.

This cauliflower soup is easy to make, creamy, and comforting and is infused with some of our favorite bold flavors: warm saffron and tangy sumac.

Store in the refrigerator for up to five days. We do not recommend freezing.

Prep time: 25 minutes
Cook time: 40 minutes
Makes 2 quarts

INGREDIENTS:

2 tablespoons extra-virgin olive oil

1 medium-size onion, chopped (about 1 cup)

2 large garlic cloves, chopped

2 pounds fresh or frozen cauliflower florets

½ teaspoon salt

¼ teaspoon freshly ground black pepper

5 cups vegetable broth or water

20 saffron threads

SUMAC OIL:

2½ tablespoons sumac

¼ cup extra-virgin olive oil

1 tablespoon freshly squeezed
   lemon juice

¼ teaspoon salt

Heat the olive oil in a large soup pot. Add the onion and garlic and cook over medium heat for 10 minutes, or until the onion is translucent.

Add the cauliflower florets, salt, and pepper and continue to cook for 10 to 12 minutes.

Add the broth or water, bring to a boil, lower the heat, and simmer for 20 minutes, or until the cauliflower is tender.

Turn off the heat. Add the saffron and stir well. Cover the pot and let the saffron steep for 20 minutes. Transfer to a blender and blend until creamy (or use an immersion blender if you have one).

Prepare the sumac oil: Whisk together all its ingredients in a small bowl until well combined.

> **TIP**
>
> Make sure to place a kitchen towel over the lid of the blender before blending the hot soup, to protect your hands in case it splashes.

Serve the soup warm with a drizzle of sumac oil.

zingy red lentil, garlic, and cilantro soup

This soup is probably the one we remember the most from our childhood. Not only because it's comforting, satisfying, and packed with flavor, but also because of the incredible aroma that engulfed the house every time our mom made it. We distinctly remember waking up to the unmistakable fragrance of garlic and cilantro sizzling on the stove.

The red lentils are slightly earthy and nutty, and packed with nutrients! This soup is both light and filling, and very easy to prepare. We like to serve it with Crispy Mini Meatless Pies (page 70) or Bulgur Wheat Tartare (page 74) to make it a complete, balanced meal. Store in the refrigerator for up to five days, or in the freezer for up to a month.

Prep time: 15 minutes
Cook time: 45 minutes
Makes 2 quarts

INGREDIENTS:

1 pound dried red lentils

2 teaspoons sea salt

¼ cup extra-virgin olive oil

4 garlic cloves, minced

1 cup chopped fresh cilantro

⅓ cup freshly squeezed lemon juice

Spread the lentils on a clean surface and remove any small stones and other debris. Transfer them to a fine-mesh colander and run them under water until it runs clear.

Bring 8 cups of water to a boil in a large soup pot. Add the salt and lentils, lower the heat to medium, and cook the lentils until tender, about 20 minutes. Skim away any white foam from the surface and discard.

While the lentils cook, heat the olive oil in a small nonstick pan. Add the garlic and cilantro and cook over medium-high heat for 3 to 4 minutes, or until the cilantro starts to turn dark green. Set aside.

Once the lentils are cooked, add the cilantro mixture and lemon juice to the pot and stir well.

Lower the heat and simmer for 20 minutes.

spinach, lentil, and bulgur soup

The inspiration for this recipe comes from a lentil and cracked wheat soup we used to eat at one of our favorite Lebanese restaurants. Our version incorporates spinach and tomato paste, for a richer, more flavorful broth. Store in the refrigerator for up to five days. We do not recommend freezing this soup.

Serve with Spicy Avocado Toast with Dukkah (page 23) or Za'atar Pita Toast with Avocado and Tomato (page 25) for a satisfying lunch.

Prep time: 30 minutes
Cook time: 1 hour
Makes 2 quarts

INGREDIENTS:

1 teaspoon extra-virgin olive oil

¼ cup tomato paste

1 medium-size onion, diced (about 1 cup)

1 cup dried French lentils, picked over and rinsed well

2 teaspoons sea salt

1 teaspoon baharat or ground allspice

1 teaspoon ground cinnamon

⅓ cup coarse bulgur wheat, rinsed

4 cups baby spinach, roughly chopped

Heat the olive oil in a large soup pot. Add the tomato paste and cook over medium-high heat for 2 to 3 minutes, stirring constantly.

Add the onion, lower the heat to medium, and cook for 5 minutes. Add ½ cup of water and continue to cook for 5 more minutes.

Add 7 cups of water and bring to a boil. Add the lentils, salt, baharat, and cinnamon. Lower the heat to low, cover the pot, and simmer for 45 minutes.

Turn off the heat and add the bulgur wheat and spinach. Stir well and let sit, covered, for 15 to 20 minutes.

creamy tomato soup with sumac eggplant croutons

This is our twist on the classic creamy tomato soup everyone loves. While the traditional recipe is usually made with butter and heavy cream to give it its creamy consistency, we use cauliflower and nondairy milk, along with some nutritional yeast for a little bit of a cheeselike taste. The crispy and slightly tangy croutons add a great contrast of texture and flavor.

Store the soup in the refrigerator for up to four days, or in the freezer for up to a month. Store the croutons separately; restore the crunch of any leftover croutons by reheating them in the oven at 350°F for ten minutes, or until crisp.

Prep time: 30 minutes
Cook time: 35 minutes
Makes 2 quarts

INGREDIENTS:

EGGPLANT CROUTONS:

Cooking spray, for pan

1 medium-size eggplant, diced

½ cup unsweetened nondairy milk

1 cup whole wheat panko bread crumbs

1 teaspoon garlic powder

1 teaspoon onion powder

¾ teaspoon salt

¼ cup all-purpose flour

1 tablespoon sumac

2 teaspoons dried thyme

⅛ teaspoon freshly ground black pepper

SOUP:

1 tablespoon extra-virgin olive oil

6 ounces tomato paste

1 tablespoon dried thyme

1 teaspoon salt

2 cups cauliflower florets

1 (28-ounce) can tomato puree

½ cup unsweetened nondairy milk

¼ cup nutritional yeast

1 tablespoon agave nectar

½ teaspoon freshly ground black pepper

EQUIPMENT:

Parchment paper

TIP

Be sure to use pureed tomatoes, since crushed would make the soup less creamy.

To prepare the eggplant croutons, preheat the oven to 375°F. Line a large baking sheet with parchment paper and coat it with cooking spray.

Prepare three large bowls and line them up on your working surface. Place the diced eggplant in the first bowl, the milk in the second bowl, and the panko in the third.

Add ½ teaspoon of the garlic powder, ½ teaspoon of the onion powder, and ¼ teaspoon of the salt to the eggplant and toss well. Add the flour and toss again.

Transfer the eggplant to the milk bowl, making sure the eggplant is covered with milk, and let it sit for a minute.

Add the sumac, dried thyme, the remaining ½ teaspoon each of garlic powder, onion powder, and salt, and the ⅛ teaspoon of pepper to the panko bowl and mix well.

Remove the eggplant from the milk, add it to the panko bowl, and toss well, so all the pieces are well coated. Transfer the eggplant to the lined baking sheet, making sure the cubes are in a single layer. Bake on the top rack of your oven for 30 to 32 minutes, or until golden brown and crispy.

While the croutons bake, prepare the soup: Heat the olive oil in a large soup pot.

Add the tomato paste, dried thyme, and ½ teaspoon of the salt and cook over medium heat for 3 minutes, stirring constantly. Add 3 cups of water and bring to a boil. Add the cauliflower, lower the heat to medium, cover, and cook for 6 to 7 minutes, or until the cauliflower is tender. Remove the pot from the heat and puree the cauliflower, using an immersion blender (see tip).

Return the pot to the heat, add the tomato puree, milk, nutritional yeast, agave nectar, remaining ½ teaspoon of salt, and pepper and continue to cook over medium heat for 2 minutes. Lower the heat to low and simmer, covered, for 15 minutes.

Serve warm, with the eggplant croutons on top.

> **TIP**
>
> If you don't have an immersion blender, transfer the soup to a regular blender and blend until smooth. Make sure to place a kitchen towel over the lid before blending the hot soup, to protect your hands in case it splashes.

quick and easy jasmine rice tomato soup

This is the tomato soup we grew up eating: very simple and easy to prepare, yet flavorful and comforting. And best of all, you most likely have all the ingredients in your pantry!

We like to serve it with Roasted Cauliflower with Green Tahini (page 173), Mushroom-Stuffed Potato Cradles (page 189), or Zucchini Fritters with Cucumber Yogurt Sauce (page 26).

Store in the refrigerator for up to four days. We do not recommend freezing this soup.

Prep time: 5 minutes
Cook time: 40 minutes
Makes 2 quarts

INGREDIENTS:

2 tablespoons extra-virgin olive oil

1 large onion, diced

1 (28-ounce) can crushed tomatoes

1½ teaspoons salt, or to taste

⅔ cup uncooked jasmine rice

Heat the olive oil in a soup pot. Add the onion and cook over medium-high heat for 5 to 7 minutes, stirring often, until translucent.

Add 6 cups of water, the tomatoes, and the salt. Bring to a boil, lower the heat to low, cover, and simmer for 20 minutes.

Add the rice, bring to a boil again, then lower the heat to low and simmer, covered, for 15 minutes, or until the rice is cooked.

simply satisfying semolina soup

Consider this soup the vegan equivalent of chicken soup: a satisfying, thick broth infused with spices that will warm you up from the inside out. Serve in small cups at the beginning of your meal, or pair with a slice of Beluga Lentil and Baba Ghanoush Toast (page 64) or Little Gem Lettuce Rainbow Salad with Warm Pomegranate Vinaigrette (page 120).

Store in the refrigerator for up to five days. We do not recommend freezing this soup.

Prep time: 30 minutes
Cook time: 25 minutes
Makes 3 quarts

INGREDIENTS:

2 tablespoons extra-virgin olive oil

3 celery stalks, cleaned and sliced

2 medium-size carrots, diced

1 medium-size onion, diced

2 garlic cloves, crushed

2 teaspoons sweet paprika

1 to 2 teaspoons Aleppo pepper, to taste

1½ teaspoons ground cumin

1 teaspoon ground turmeric

1 teaspoon ground coriander

1 teaspoon salt

1 (28-ounce) can diced tomatoes

6 cups water or vegetable broth

1 (15-ounce) can chickpeas or cannellini beans, drained and rinsed

½ cup semolina flour

2 to 4 tablespoons freshly squeezed lemon juice, to taste

1 cup chopped fresh cilantro

Heat the olive oil in a large soup pot. Add the celery, carrots, onion, garlic, sweet paprika, Aleppo pepper, cumin, turmeric, coriander, and salt and cook over medium-high heat for 2 to 3 minutes, stirring often, or until fragrant.

Add the canned tomatoes, the water or broth, and the chickpeas or cannellini beans. Bring to a boil, lower the heat to low, cover, and simmer for 20 minutes.

Add the semolina while stirring constantly. Add the lemon juice and cilantro, bring to a boil, and turn off the heat. Let the soup sit, covered, for 15 minutes.

SPICED TOASTED BULGUR SALAD
WITH TAHINI DRESSING

5

big-enough-to-share salads

While growing up, we never ate a boring salad. We never used bottled dressing, either; it was always homemade! As you will discover as you explore this chapter, jazzing up a salad doesn't take much. We are used to eating family style, where we share salads as part of the main meal and serve all dishes at once. However, some of these salads can also stand alone as a hearty meal. In some of the recipes we've added grains or beans for protein. In others, we began with a Western base and added Middle Eastern ingredients, such as sumac, silan (date syrup), and bulgur wheat. Tangy and flavorful homemade dressings add the final touch. This is how we make salads, Middle Eastern style.

quinoa and black bean tabbouleh

Traditionally made with bulgur wheat, tabbouleh is probably one of the most pop-ular Middle Eastern salads. This version uses quinoa instead of bulgur wheat and black beans to make it more filling and nutritious by adding fiber, protein, vitamins, and minerals. Serve with a cup of Saffron-Infused Cauliflower Soup with Sumac Oil (page 93) for a hearty lunch or light dinner.

Store the tabbouleh in an airtight container in the refrigerator for up to three days.

Prep time: 1 hour 15 minutes (includes refrigeration time)
Cook time: 20 minutes
Makes 4 to 6 servings

INGREDIENTS:

2½ cups cooked quinoa

20 yellow grape tomatoes, quartered

20 red grape tomatoes, quartered

4 scallions, sliced

4 cups chopped fresh parsley

1 (15-ounce) can black beans, drained and rinsed

½ to ¾ cup freshly squeezed lemon juice, to taste

¼ cup plus 2 tablespoons extra-virgin olive oil

1 teaspoon salt

Combine the cooked quinoa, tomatoes, scallions, parsley, and black beans in a large bowl. Add the lemon juice, olive oil, and salt and mix well. Cover the bowl and refrigerate for 1 hour before serving.

HOW TO COOK QUINOA
Makes about 2½ cups quinoa

INGREDIENTS:
2 teaspoons extra-virgin olive oil
1 cup uncooked quinoa, rinsed
½ teaspoon salt

Heat the olive oil in a medium-size saucepan. Add the quinoa and cook over medium heat for 1 to 2 minutes, stirring often, so it's well coated with the oil. Add 1¼ cups of water and the salt. Bring to a boil, cover, and simmer for 15 to 20 minutes, or until all the water has been absorbed and the quinoa is tender but not mushy. Remove from the heat, let sit, covered, for 5 minutes, then fluff with a fork.

cannellini bean and farro salad

During the summer months, our mom would often make a white bean, bell pepper, and sweet onion salad for lunch. Simply dressed with lemon juice, a drizzle of olive oil, and salt, it became one of our summer staples. Our version adds farro, an ancient grain similar to wheat that has been eaten in Mediterranean and Middle Eastern countries for thousands of years, to make it heartier and nutritionally balanced. Farro is high in fiber, B vitamins, iron, and magnesium, as well as being a great source of plant-based protein. It has a slightly chewy texture and nutty flavor, and it's a great addition to soups, salads, and stews.

Store in an airtight container for up to three days.

Prep time: 10 minutes
Cook time: 30 minutes
Makes 4 to 6 servings

INGREDIENTS:

- 2 tablespoons plus 1 teaspoon extra-virgin olive oil
- 1 cup pearled farro, rinsed
- 1 teaspoon salt
- 1 (15-ounce) can cannellini beans, drained and rinsed
- 1 red bell pepper, seeded and diced large
- 1 green bell pepper, seeded and diced large
- 3 scallions, white and green parts, sliced
- 3 tablespoons freshly squeezed lemon juice

Heat 1 teaspoon of the olive oil in a small saucepan. Add the farro and cook over medium heat for 1 minute, stirring constantly. Add 1¼ cups of water and ½ teaspoon of the salt and bring to a boil. Lower the heat to low, cover, and cook for 28 to 30 minutes, or until most of the water has become absorbed and the farro is tender. Remove from the heat and set aside to cool.

Once the farro has cooled, transfer it to a large bowl. Add the beans, bell peppers, scallions, remaining 2 tablespoons of olive oil, the lemon juice, and the remaining ½ teaspoon of salt and toss well. Refrigerate until ready to serve.

lentil fattoush with mint and sumac

Fattoush is a traditional Middle Eastern salad made with romaine lettuce, fresh mint, and toasted or fried pita bread. We give this classic dish an extra pop of flavor by adding some tasty za'atar to the bread, and an extra protein boost by adding lentils to the salad. We recommend using beluga lentils, because they keep their shape better than the brown variety.

The best part of *fattoush* is, without a doubt, the pita croutons. So, we suggest you make extra to add to other dishes or simply enjoy as a snack!

Prep time: 15 minutes
Cook time: 30 minutes
Makes 4 to 6 servings

INGREDIENTS:

1 to 1¼ teaspoons salt, to taste

¾ cup dried black beluga lentils, picked over and rinsed

¼ cup za'atar

¼ cup plus 2 tablespoons extra-virgin olive oil

2 whole wheat pita pockets, opened and separated along the edge into 4 disks

2 romaine lettuce hearts, chopped

4 Persian cucumbers or 1 English cucumber, diced

2 vine-ripened tomatoes, chopped

1 medium-size red bell pepper, seeded and diced

1 medium-size orange bell pepper, seeded and diced

1 medium-size yellow bell pepper, seeded and diced

1 cup chopped fresh parsley

A small bunch of fresh mint, chopped

3 to 4 tablespoons freshly squeezed lemon juice, to taste

1 tablespoon sumac

> TIP
>
> The most important step when making this salad is to dress it right before serving, so the pita stays crunchy.

Preheat the oven to 375°F. Line a large baking sheet with aluminum foil.

Combine 6 cups of water and ½ teaspoon of the salt in a large saucepan and bring to a boil over high heat. Add the rinsed lentils, lower the heat to medium, and cook, uncovered, for 20 to 25 minutes, or until the lentils are tender but slightly firm. Drain well and set aside to cool.

Combine the za'atar and 2 tablespoons of the olive oil in a small bowl and mix well. Spread on each pita disk.

Transfer the pita disks to the lined baking sheet and bake for 7 minutes, or until golden brown. Remove from the oven, let cool for a few minutes, then break the disks into medium-size pieces (about 16 pieces each). Set the croutons aside until you are ready to use them.

Combine all the vegetables and the parsley and mint in a large bowl. Right before serving, add the pita croutons, the remaining ¼ cup of olive oil, the lemon juice to taste, sumac, and remaining salt and toss well.

crunchy crudités salad with spiced chickpeas

Our family is almost obsessed with anything crunchy. Whether it's snacks, desserts, or main meals, we are always looking for that crunch element—which makes this salad one of our absolute favorites. Crisp, colorful veggies are topped with flavor-packed, warm spiced chickpeas and tossed with creamy, tangy tahini dressing. Serve with Spicy Avocado Toast with Dukkah (page 23) for a balanced, satisfying lunch.

Prep time: 10 minutes
Cook time: 5 minutes
Makes 4 servings

INGREDIENTS:

6 to 7 celery stalks, sliced (2¼ cups)

3 to 4 radishes, thinly sliced

1 medium-size watermelon radish, cut in half and thinly sliced

3 rainbow carrots, peeled and thinly sliced

1 tablespoon extra-virgin olive oil

1 (15-ounce) can chickpeas, drained and rinsed

1 tablespoon Good-on-Everything Spice Mix (page 131)

⅛ to ¼ teaspoon salt, to taste

Tahini Dressing (page 134)

Combine the vegetables in a medium-size bowl. Toss well and set aside.

Heat the olive oil in a medium-size skillet. Add the chickpeas, spice mix, and salt and toss well, making sure the chickpeas are well coated with the spices. Cook over medium heat for 3 to 5 minutes, or until warm.

Add the warm chickpeas to the vegetables, pour on the desired amount of tahini dressing, and toss well.

belgian endive salad with pomegranate and pumpkin seeds

A lot of people shy away from endive, mostly because of its slightly bitter flavor. That, however, can be easily disguised by preparing the greens properly, and pairing them with the right ingredients and dressings. As an example, using straight lemon juice will enhance the bitterness, but when endive is combined with a little bit of vinegar and a sweet element, it enhances the slightly herbal taste and sweetness of the greens.

This salad can be served as a light appetizer before the main meal. We recommend serving it freshly made.

Prep time: 10 minutes
Makes 4 servings

INGREDIENTS:

4 Belgian endives, sliced

1½ cups pomegranate seeds

1 cup peeled and shredded carrot

1 cup fresh or frozen corn kernels (thaw if frozen)

¼ cup raw or roasted pumpkin seeds

Maple Mustard Vinaigrette (page 139)

Combine all the salad ingredients, except the dressing, in a large bowl. Add the dressing and toss well. Transfer to a serving platter before serving.

little gem lettuce rainbow salad with warm pomegranate vinaigrette

Little Gem lettuce hearts are a cross between butter and romaine lettuces, compact and crisp with a sweet, almost buttery taste. Very popular in Spain, they are served in the best restaurants all over the country with just a simple vinaigrette, or topped with a few anchovy fillets.

In this simple but flavor-packed salad, the little gems are the star, with the Warm Pomegranate Vinaigrette (page 138) enhancing their natural sweetness and adding a Middle Eastern touch.

Prep time: 10 minutes
Makes 6 servings

INGREDIENTS:

3 Little Gem lettuce hearts, cut in half lengthwise

1½ cups peeled, shredded carrot

6 ounces jarred roasted red peppers, diced

1 cup fresh or frozen corn (thaw if frozen)

5 to 6 canned hearts of palm, sliced

Warm Pomegranate Vinaigrette (page 138)

Arrange the lettuce on a large platter. Top with the carrot, roasted peppers, hearts of palm, and corn. Serve with the warm pomegranate vinaigrette.

spiced toasted bulgur salad with tahini dressing

Bulgur wheat adds a wonderful chewy, hearty bite to salads. We soak the bulgur in boiling water to soften it a little bit, and then we sauté it with our Good-on-Everything Spice Mix (page 131).

For this recipe, we use coarse bulgur, which you can find in most grocery stores. You can use regular radishes if you can't find the watermelon variety.

Prep time: 30 minutes (includes soaking time)
Cook time: 5 minutes
Makes 4 to 6 servings

INGREDIENTS:

½ cup coarse bulgur wheat

1 cup boiling water

1 tablespoon extra-virgin olive oil

2 teaspoons Good-on-Everything Spice Mix (page 131)

¼ teaspoon salt

2 romaine lettuce hearts, chopped

1 pint grape tomatoes, sliced in half

4 to 5 Persian cucumbers, sliced

1 watermelon radish, sliced

1 cup chopped fresh parsley

Tahini Dressing (page 134)

Rinse the bulgur wheat in a fine-mesh strainer. Transfer to a heatproof bowl and pour the boiling water over the bulgur. Cover and let sit for 15 to 20 minutes. Drain well.

Heat the olive oil in a medium-size skillet. Add the bulgur wheat, spice mix, and salt and toss well, so the spices coat the bulgur. Cook over high heat for 5 minutes, tossing often, until fragrant.

Combine the romaine lettuce, tomatoes, cucumbers, radish, parsley, and cooked bulgur wheat in a large bowl. Right before serving, add the tahini dressing and toss well.

wheat berry, fig, and pistachio salad

Wheat berries are whole wheat kernels with a wonderful nutty taste and chewy texture. High in protein and fiber and rich in B vitamins and minerals, they are a great base for hearty salads and soups.

This recipe is a beautiful combination of flavors and textures: sweet figs and tomatoes, chewy wheat berries, creamy avocado, and crunchy pistachios tossed with tangy lemon juice and fruity olive oil.

Store it in the refrigerator for up to four days.

Prep time: 10 minutes
Cook time: 40 minutes
Makes 4 to 6 servings

INGREDIENTS:

1 cup uncooked wheat berries

½ teaspoon plus ⅛ teaspoon salt

4 fresh figs, sliced

3 red cherry tomatoes, sliced in half

3 yellow cherry tomatoes, sliced in half

1 Hass avocado, peeled, pitted, and diced

¼ cup shelled pistachios, roughly chopped

¼ cup freshly squeezed lemon juice

2 tablespoons olive oil

TIP

During the colder months, you can use persimmons instead of figs.

Combine the wheat berries with 3 cups of water and ⅛ teaspoon of the salt in a large saucepan. Bring to a boil, lower the heat to low, cover, and simmer for 35 to 40 minutes, or until the wheat berries are tender but slightly chewy (check them after 35 minutes and continue to cook if they are not done). Drain and set aside to cool.

To assemble the salad, combine the cooked wheat berries, sliced figs, tomatoes, diced avocado. and pistachios in a large bowl and toss well. Add the lemon juice, olive oil, and remaining ½ teaspoon of salt and mix well. Refrigerate until ready to serve.

GOOD-ON-EVERYTHING SPICE MIX
(ABOVE) AND *DUKKAH* (LEFT)

6

dressings and condiments

Homemade dressings are very quick and easy to prepare. Unlike the store-bought varieties, you can control the ingredients that go in them, as well as the flavor profiles. You can customize them however you like! We personally prefer our dressing on the tart side, so we are pretty generous with the amount of lemon juice and vinegar we use. You can taste the dressings as you prepare them, and adjust the ingredients until you find your own balance.

The same goes for spice mixes. You can add more of your favorite ingredients, and omit the ones you don't like so much. It's a wonderful way to get creative and have fun with your food!

dukkah

Dukkah is a condiment of Egyptian origin that combines herbs, nuts, and spices; you can customize it by using your favorite ingredients. It can be added to pretty much everything, from hummus, to salads, to—you guessed it—toast! To prepare the *dukkah*, you will need a coffee or spice grinder, which we truly believe is a worthwhile investment. Our blend is nutty and slightly smoky, with a subtle licorice taste that comes from the fennel seeds.

This recipe makes 1¼ cups of *dukkah* and it can be stored in the refrigerator for up to three months.

Prep time: 10 minutes
Cook time: 2 minutes
Makes 1¼ cups

INGREDIENTS:

¼ cup fennel seeds

1½ tablespoons coriander seeds

1½ tablespoons cumin seeds

¼ cup toasted sesame seeds

¼ cup black sesame seeds

¼ cup roasted shelled pistachios, roughly chopped

¼ cup toasted sunflower seeds, roughly chopped

1½ teaspoons salt

To prepare the *dukkah*, combine the fennel, coriander, and cumin seeds in a small bowl. Place a 10-inch skillet on the stove over high heat. Add the seed mixture and toast for 2 minutes, or until fragrant, stirring often. Transfer the seeds to a bowl and let them cool slightly.

Once the seeds have cooled, grind them finely. Transfer to a bowl and add both sesame seeds and the pistachios, sunflower seeds, and salt.

good-on-everything spice mix

This combination of spices is the one we use the most when we cook. It adds a slightly smoky, savory flavor and a beautiful color to anything from vegetables, beans, and proteins to soups and stews.

Makes ¾ cup

INGREDIENTS:

¼ cup sweet paprika

2½ tablespoons ground turmeric

2 tablespoons ground cumin

2 tablespoons Aleppo pepper

1 teaspoon ground coriander

1 teaspoon salt (optional)

½ teaspoon freshly ground black
    pepper

Combine all the ingredients in a medium-size bowl and mix well. Store in an airtight glass jar for up to three months.

homemade pomegranate molasses

If you can't find store-bought pomegranate molasses, you can make your own using just three ingredients! It's thick, sweet, and tangy and enhances the flavor of many dishes, especially stuffed vegetables.

Makes 2¼ cups

INGREDIENTS:

6 cups pomegranate juice

1 cup sugar

⅓ cup freshly squeezed lemon juice

Combine all the ingredients in a large saucepan and bring to a boil. Lower the temperature to a low boil and cook, uncovered, for 2 hours, or until the liquid has reduced to about one third. Keep an eye on it, so it doesn't overflow.

Remove from the heat, let cool, and transfer to a glass jar with a tight lid. The molasses will thicken once cooled.

Store in the refrigerator for up to six months.

basic tahini sauce

A staple in Middle Eastern cooking, this tangy and nutty sauce brings great flavor to pretty much anything you add it to! It's traditionally served with such dishes as Bulgur Wheat Pie (page 199) and Bulgur Wheat Patties (page 72), but it can be used as a dressing for salads and vegetables. We love to just dip fresh pita bread in it!
Makes 1 cup

INGREDIENTS:

½ cup tahini

¼ cup freshly squeezed lemon juice,
   plus 2 tablespoons (optional)

½ teaspoon salt

Whisk together the tahini, ¼ cup of lemon juice, and salt in a small bowl until thickened. Add water, 1 tablespoon at a time, whisking constantly until creamy (should be no more than 4 tablespoons). Taste and add up to 2 tablespoons more lemon juice, if needed.

Store in the refrigerator for up to five days; the sauce will thicken with the cold, so bring it to room temperature just before using.

tahini dressing

A slightly sweeter, thinner version of the Basic Tahini Sauce (page 133), with a hint of olive oil, this dressing adds a wonderful nutty, rich flavor to salads and roasted vegetables.

Makes 1 cup

INGREDIENTS:

⅓ cup plus 1 tablespoon tahini

⅓ cup freshly squeezed lemon juice

1 tablespoon extra-virgin olive oil

1 teaspoon agave nectar

¼ teaspoon salt, or to taste

Combine all the ingredients in a blender, add ⅓ cup of water, and blend until smooth. Refrigerate until ready to use. This dressing will thicken when cold. Bring to room temperature before using, or for a thinner consistency, just add a little bit of water and whisk or shake well. This will keep in the fridge for five days.

grainy mustard balsamic vinaigrette

This is a basic go-to vinaigrette. You can dress simple greens and grains with it or even use it as marinade for tofu, vegetables, and so forth.

Makes 1 cup

INGREDIENTS:

¼ cup balsamic vinegar

¼ cup extra-virgin olive oil

2 tablespoons whole-grain mustard

1 tablespoon spicy brown mustard

1 tablespoon agave nectar

⅛ to ¼ teaspoon of salt

Place all the ingredients, plus 3 tablespoons of water, in a glass jar with a lid. Close it tightly and shake vigorously until all the ingredients are well combined. Refrigerate until ready to use. This dressing will keep for five days in the fridge.

cumin dressing

This smoky, tangy dressing pairs beautifully with cooked grains and beans, and with assertive vegetables, such as beets or cabbage. The brown mustard adds a hint of spice and creaminess.

Makes ½ cup

INGREDIENTS:

¼ cup freshly squeezed lemon juice

2 tablespoons extra-virgin olive oil

2 tablespoons spicy brown mustard

1 teaspoon pure maple syrup

1 teaspoon ground cumin

⅛ teaspoon salt, or to taste

Place all the ingredients in a glass jar with a lid. Close it tightly and shake vigorously until all the ingredients are well combined. Refrigerate until ready to use. This will keep in the fridge for five days.

silan tahini dressing

Silan gives this dressing a unique, rich sweetness that pairs particularly well with roasted eggplant. We highly recommend giving it a try! If silan isn't available, you can use other sweeteners, such as maple syrup, agave nectar, or coconut molasses, but take into consideration that the flavor will change significantly.

Makes 2/3 cup

INGREDIENTS:

3 tablespoons silan

2 tablespoons tahini

1/3 to 1/2 cup freshly squeezed lemon
    juice, to taste

1/8 teaspoon salt

Place all the ingredients in a glass jar with a lid. Close it tightly and shake vigorously until all the ingredients are well combined. Refrigerate until ready to use. This will thicken when cold, so bring to room temperature before using, or add water to thin to your desired consistency. The dressing will keep in the fridge for five days.

warm pomegranate vinaigrette

The reduced pomegranate juice gives this dressing a wonderful balance of sweet and tart flavors. The addition of olive oil at the end makes it rich and silky. Serve it warm over salads or roasted vegetables.

Cook time: 10 minutes

Makes 1 cup

INGREDIENTS:

1 cup pomegranate juice

1 small shallot, minced

1 tablespoon whole-grain mustard

1 tablespoon Dijon mustard

2 teaspoons pure maple syrup

2 tablespoons extra-virgin olive oil

Combine all the ingredients, except the olive oil, in a small saucepan and bring to a boil.

Lower the heat to low and simmer for 10 minutes.

Remove from the heat, let the dressing cool slightly, and whisk in the olive oil until completely incorporated. This dressing will keep in the fridge for five days.

maple mustard vinaigrette

This is another go-to vinaigrette and pairs well with any kind of salad, be it vegetables, grain, or bean based. It has an assertive, peppery flavor from the grainy and Dijon mustards, balanced by a hint of sweetness from the maple syrup.
Makes 1 cup

INGREDIENTS:

2 tablespoons whole-grain mustard

2 tablespoons Dijon mustard

2 tablespoons pure maple syrup

3 tablespoons red wine vinegar

¼ cup extra-virgin olive oil

1 tablespoon freshly squeezed lemon juice

¼ teaspoon salt

⅛ teaspoon freshly ground black pepper

Place all the ingredients in a glass jar with a lid. Close it tightly and shake vigorously until well combined. Refrigerate until ready to use. The dressing will keep in the fridge for five days.

FAVA BEAN AND FRIED
ARTICHOKE BASMATI RICE

7

kicked-up rice

We didn't know that making rice was such a challenge until we came to the United States. Our mom always made it in twenty minutes and it came out perfectly. Cooks in the Middle East excel at this fundamental ingredient, using it as a blank canvas for wildly flavorful dishes filled with herbs, dried fruit, nuts, and vegetables. These recipes will show you how to prepare rice in extremely delicious ways, so your plain old boring steamed rice will go from blah to ta-da in no time!

lebanese white rice with vermicelli

This almost foolproof rice can be used as a base or side for any of your favorite dishes. It's our equivalent to plain, steamed white rice, but as you will discover, with a lot more flavor. The addition of vermicelli (very thin, short noodles) gives this simple rice a slightly nutty touch. Try to resist the temptation to taste it right off the stove, or you might end up eating the whole pan! You will love it served with our Quinoa Harissa Meatless Meatballs with Artichokes in Aromatic Turmeric Broth (page 195) and Caramelized Baby Okra in Tomato and Pomegranate Molasses Sauce (page 168).

Prep time: 15 minutes
Cook time: 20 minutes
Makes 4 servings

INGREDIENTS:

1 cup uncooked jasmine or basmati rice

1 tablespoon neutral-flavor oil (such as sunflower, avocado, or grapeseed)

½ cup vermicelli noodles

1 teaspoon salt

Rinse the rice with warm water until it runs clear. Drain well and set aside.

Heat the oil in a deep, nonstick skillet with a lid. Add the vermicelli and cook over medium heat for 2 to 3 minutes, stirring constantly, or until golden brown. Add 1½ cups of water, the rinsed rice, and salt and bring to a boil. Lower the heat to low, cover the skillet, and simmer for 20 minutes.

Remove from the heat and let sit, covered, for 10 to 15 minutes. Fluff with a fork and serve warm.

> TIP
>
> Make sure to keep an eye on the vermicelli while they cook, as they can burn easily.
>
>
>
> Store the rice in the refrigerator for up to two days.

wild rice mjadra

Our take on this classic Middle Eastern dish incorporates wild rice and sautéed on-ions, as opposed to fried, for a healthier version. We also cook the rice, lentils, and onions separately, and then mix them together right before serving. This is a fool-proof method to prevent the *mjadra* from becoming mushy.

Traditionally, this dish is served topped with a cucumber yogurt sauce, which we made using nondairy yogurt (see Zucchini Fritters with Cucumber Yogurt Sauce, page 26). While we were growing up, our dad always ate it with his favorite Spicy Israeli Salsa (page 62), made with freshly picked tomatoes and cucumbers from his garden.

Store in the refrigerator for up to four days.

Prep time: 10 minutes
Cook time: 50 minutes
Makes 6 to 8 servings

INGREDIENTS:

WILD RICE:

½ cup uncooked wild rice

½ teaspoon salt

LENTILS:

1 cup dried French green lentils, picked over and rinsed well

½ teaspoon salt

WHITE RICE:

1 cup uncooked basmati rice

1 teaspoon salt

SAUTÉED ONIONS:

2 tablespoons extra-virgin olive oil

1 large onion, sliced

¼ teaspoon salt

⅛ teaspoon freshly ground black pepper

1 tablespoon pomegranate molasses (see page 132 for homemade)

Cucumber Yogurt Sauce (page 26) or Spicy Israeli Salsa (page 62), to serve

Prepare the wild rice: Bring 2 cups of water to a boil in a medium-size saucepan over high heat. Add the wild rice and salt. Bring again to a boil, lower the heat to low, and simmer, covered, for 40 to 45 minutes, or until tender. Remove from the heat, drain well, and set aside.

Prepare the lentils: Bring 4 cups of water to a boil in a large saucepan over high heat. Add the lentils and salt. Lower the heat to medium and cook, uncovered, for 18 to 20 minutes, or until the lentils are soft but not mushy. Remove from the heat, drain well, and set aside.

Prepare the basmati rice: In a medium-size saucepan, bring 1½ cups of water to a boil in a separate medium-size saucepan over high heat. Add the basmati rice and salt. Return to a boil, lower the heat to low, and simmer, covered, for 20 minutes, until the water has been absorbed and the rice is tender. Remove from the heat and set aside, covered.

Prepare the onion: Heat the olive oil in a large, nonstick skillet. Add the sliced onion, salt, and pepper, and cook over high heat for 5 minutes, stirring often. Lower the heat to medium-low and cook for 15 minutes. Add the pomegranate molasses and continue to cook for another 5 minutes, or until the onion turns dark golden brown.

Assemble the *mjadra*: Combine the cooked wild and basmati rice, the cooked lentils, and the onion in a large bowl, and toss well. Serve warm, topped with Cucumber Yogurt Sauce or Spicy Israeli Salsa.

nutty green rice

Fresh herbs are a great way to infuse flavor into rice. If you are not a cilantro lover, you can omit it and increase the amount of parsley and dill by half a cup each, and add a few extra mint leaves.

Sautéing the rice before adding the water helps keep it loose and fluffy. We suggest serving it freshly made, but it can be stored in the refrigerator for up to two days.

Serve it with Tempeh-Stuffed Zucchini in Mint Tomato Sauce (page 175), or alongside roasted vegetables.

Prep time: 15 minutes
Cook time: 18 minutes
Makes 4 to 6 servings

INGREDIENTS:

1 cup tightly packed fresh parsley

1 cup tightly packed fresh cilantro

1 cup tightly packed fresh dill

12 fresh mint leaves

1 sprig of fresh rosemary

2 garlic cloves

2 tablespoons extra-virgin olive oil

1 teaspoon salt

1½ cups uncooked jasmine rice

2⅓ cups boiling water

TOPPING:

1 teaspoon olive oil

¼ cup chopped walnuts

¼ cup pine nuts

Combine the parsley, cilantro, dill, mint, rosemary, garlic, 1 tablespoon of the olive oil, and ½ teaspoon of the salt in a food processor. Pulse until all the ingredients come together to form a paste.

Heat the remaining tablespoon of olive oil in a deep, nonstick skillet with a lid. Add the herbs and cook over medium heat for a little bit under a minute, stirring constantly. Add the rice and continue to cook for 1 minute. Add the boiling water and remaining ½ teaspoon of salt and stir well. Lower the heat to low, cover the skillet, and simmer for 18 to 20 minutes, or until most of the water has been absorbed.

Remove from the heat and let sit, covered, for 10 minutes.

In the meantime, prepare the topping: Heat the olive oil in a small skillet. Add the walnuts and pine nuts and cook over medium heat for 2 minutes, stirring constantly, or until the nuts start to brown.

Serve the rice warm, topped with the walnuts and pine nuts.

wild mushroom rice

When we were kids, our parents used to take us to a beautiful restaurant twenty minutes outside of Barcelona that specialized in Catalan cuisine. It was located on a little hill off the Mediterranean coast, on a huge property in a heavily wooded area. The chef and his wife owned the place, and we ate there so often that we got the VIP treatment every time.

Besides being an amazing chef, the owner of the restaurant was also an expert mushroom forager. Not an easy task, considering the numerous varieties of poisonous mushrooms that grow out there! We got to discover and enjoy all kinds of wild and unique mushrooms at a very early age, and now we absolutely love cooking with them. For this recipe, we chose some of the more locally available mushrooms, but you can use your favorite varieties—no matter which kind you use, this rice is earthy and hearty, and pairs beautifully with dishes such as our Roasted Cauliflower with Green Tahini (page 173) and Belgian Endive Salad with Pomegranate and Pumpkin Seeds (page 119). For a more intense flavor, use mushroom broth to cook the rice; it is available in most grocery stores.

Prep time: 10 minutes
Cook time: 30 minutes
Makes 4 to 6 servings

INGREDIENTS:

2 tablespoons extra-virgin olive oil

1½ cups uncooked basmati rice

2⅓ cups mushroom or vegetable broth

¾ teaspoon salt

2 garlic cloves, crushed

1 cup shiitake mushrooms, sliced

1 cup baby bella mushrooms, sliced

½ cup chanterelle mushrooms, roughly chopped

½ cup baby oyster mushrooms, roughly chopped

3 scallions, white and green parts, sliced

½ teaspoon smoked paprika

⅛ teaspoon freshly ground black pepper

Heat 1 tablespoon of the olive oil in a deep, nonstick skillet with a lid. Add the rice and cook over medium heat for 2 minutes, stirring constantly, or until fragrant. Add the broth and ½ teaspoon of the salt, stir well, and bring to a boil. Lower the heat to low, cover the skillet, and simmer for 18 to 20 minutes, or until most of the water has been absorbed.

Remove from the heat and let sit, covered, for 10 minutes.

In the meantime, heat the remaining tablespoon of olive oil in a large, nonstick skillet. Add the crushed garlic and cook over medium heat for 1 minute, stirring constantly. Add the mushrooms and scallions and continue to cook for 5 to 6 minutes, or until most of the water has evaporated. Add the paprika, remaining ¼ teaspoon of salt, and the pepper and cook for 2 more minutes.

Combine the cooked rice and mushrooms in a large bowl and toss well. Serve warm.

cumin jasmine rice with almonds, walnuts, and cashews

Smoky cumin, slow-cooked sweet onions, and rich toasted nuts add so much flavor to this dish, you will never look at rice the same way again. It's the perfect accompaniment for our Roasted Cauliflower with Green Tahini (page 173) or served alongside some plain Quinoa Harissa Meatless Meatballs (page 195). This dish is best when served fresh, but you can store the leftovers in the refrigerator for up to two days.

Prep time: 20 minutes
Cook time: 1 hour 30 minutes
Makes 4 to 6 servings

INGREDIENTS:

¼ cup olive oil

3 large sweet onions, sliced

1¾ teaspoons salt

1¾ teaspoons ground cumin

1½ cups uncooked jasmine rice

2 teaspoons neutral-flavor oil (such as sunflower, avocado, or grapeseed)

¼ cup sliced raw almonds

¼ cup raw walnuts, chopped

¼ cup raw cashews, roughly chopped

chopped parsley and pomegranate seeds, for garnish (optional)

Heat the olive oil in a deep, medium-size skillet with a lid. Add the onions and cook over medium-low heat for 1 hour, or until golden brown, stirring frequently (you might need to add some water during the cooking process to prevent them from burning).

Add 2⅓ cups of water, and the salt and cumin and bring to a boil. Add the rice and stir well. Bring to a boil again, lower the heat to low, cover, and simmer for 25 minutes.

TIME-SAVING TIP

Cook the onions one to two days in advance, and refrigerate them until they are ready to be used.

Uncover the skillet and gently fluff up the rice with a fork. Replace the lid and remove the skillet from the heat. Let sit for 10 minutes.

In the meantime, heat the neutral-flavor oil in a separate skillet over medium heat. Add the almonds, walnuts, and cashews and toast them for 2 to 3 minutes, stirring constantly, or until golden brown, watching them carefully to prevent them from burning.

Once the rice is ready, transfer it to a large serving platter and top with the toasted nuts. Garnish with parsley and pomegranate seeds, if using.

sweet and savory basmati rice with carrots and raisins

Our mom makes this delicious rice dish every year for Rosh Hashanah, the Jewish new year. An absolute crowd-pleaser, it has wonderful balance of sweet and savory ingredients, as well as a stunning color. The toasted almonds add a contrast of texture and a slight nutty flavor. It pairs beautifully with our Stuffed Grape Leaves with Figs and Blood Orange (page 178).

Store in the refrigerator for up to two days.

Prep time: 20 minutes
Cook time: 30 minutes
Makes 6 to 8 servings

INGREDIENTS:

2 tablespoons plus ½ teaspoon neutral-flavor oil (such as sunflower, grapeseed, or avocado)

1 medium-size onion, sliced

4 cups shredded carrot

¾ cup raisins

2 teaspoons salt

1½ cups uncooked white basmati rice

⅓ cup raw slivered almonds

Heat 2 tablespoons of the oil in a large, deep skillet with a lid. Add the onion and cook over medium heat for 5 minutes, or until translucent.

Add the shredded carrot and continue to cook for about 7 minutes.

Add 2⅓ cups of water and the raisins and salt and bring to a boil. Add the rice and stir well. Bring to a boil again, lower the heat to low, cover, and simmer for 25 minutes.

In the meantime, heat the remaining ½ teaspoon of oil in a small skillet. Add the slivered almonds and toast over medium heat for 3 to 4 minutes, stirring constantly, or until golden brown. Set aside.

Once the rice is done, remove from the heat and uncover the skillet. Gently fluff up the rice with a fork. Replace the lid and let sit for 10 minutes. Sprinkle the toasted almonds on top before serving.

fava bean and fried artichoke basmati rice

Artichokes are one of our favorite vegetables. Cleaning them, however, is quite a laborious, time-consuming process. Frozen artichoke bottoms are just as delicious and will save you a lot of time. You can also use canned, which are available in most grocery stores. Make sure you dry them very well before dropping them into the hot oil, to keep it from splashing.

Frying the artichokes brings out their natural sweetness and adds a wonderful crunch to the rice. The fava beans are earthy and hearty and make the rice a complete dish.

Prep time: 20 minutes
Cook time: 30 minutes
Makes 4 to 6 servings

INGREDIENTS:

2 tablespoons extra-virgin olive oil

1 cup chopped fresh cilantro

4 garlic cloves, sliced

14 ounces frozen fava beans, thawed

1½ cups uncooked basmati rice

2 teaspoons salt

¼ cup neutral-flavor oil (such as sunflower, avocado, or grapeseed)

14 ounces frozen artichoke bottoms, thawed and sliced, or 14 ounces canned, drained and patted dry

¼ teaspoon freshly ground black pepper

Zest of 1 large lemon

Freshly squeezed lemon juice (optional)

Heat the olive oil in a large, deep skillet with a lid. Add the cilantro and garlic and cook over medium heat for 2 to 3 minutes. Add the fava beans and continue to cook for 3 to 4 minutes, or until warm.

Add the rice, mix well, and cook for 3 to 4 minutes. Add 2⅓ cups of water and 1½ teaspoons of the salt. Bring to a boil, cover the skillet, and lower the heat to low. Simmer for 20 minutes, or until the water is absorbed.

In the meantime, line a large plate with paper towels. Heat the neutral-flavor oil in a large skillet. Add the artichoke slices, remaining ½ teaspoon of salt, and the pepper. Cook over medium-high heat for 3 to 5 minutes per side, or until golden brown. Using a slotted spoon, transfer the fried artichokes to the lined plate, so the paper towels absorb the excess oil.

Once the rice is done, remove the skillet from the heat and remove the lid. Gently fluff up the rice with a fork, replace the lid, and let sit for 10 to 15 minutes.

Add the artichokes to the rice (you can reserve some to use for garnish) and toss well. Top with lemon zest right before serving. You can also add a squeeze of lemon juice.

8

the main event

If you're vegan or even vegetarian, chances are you've been asked this question at least once: "You don't eat meat, so where do you get your protein from?" Hmm . . . let's see . . . beans, grains, seeds, nuts, sprouts . . . Sounds like plenty of sources, don't you think? Interesting how people are only interested in your protein intake when they find out you don't eat meat! Most people also assume that a vegan diet has to be boring and pretty much flavorless. A Middle Eastern twist is all you need to prove them wrong. The combination of spices and intense flavors will elevate any dish to a point where meat won't be missed . . . even by the most skeptical carnivores.

couscous with caramelized butternut squash

If you really want to impress your guests, this dish is exactly what you need. The couscous is rubbed (yes, rubbed!) with cumin, turmeric, and sweet paprika, while the onions and squash slowly caramelize for an enticing balance of sweet and savory. The topper? Toasted nuts add the perfect touch of crunch.

Prep time: 15 minutes
Cook time: 1 hour
Makes 8 to 10 servings

INGREDIENTS:

ROASTED SQUASH:

1 large butternut squash, seeded, peeled, and diced large

3 tablespoons extra-virgin olive oil

1 teaspoon salt

¼ cup plus 2 tablespoons light brown sugar

CARAMELIZED ONIONS:

3 tablespoons extra-virgin olive oil

2 large sweet onions, sliced thinly

1 teaspoon salt

2 tablespoons light brown sugar

5 ounces peeled and roasted chestnuts, halved

⅔ cup dried cherries

COUSCOUS:

2 cups uncooked whole wheat couscous

1 teaspoon salt

1 teaspoon sweet paprika

½ teaspoon ground turmeric

¼ teaspoon ground cumin

2 tablespoons vegetable oil

2 cups boiling water

NUT TOPPING:

1 teaspoon vegetable oil

⅓ cup sliced almonds

⅓ cup shelled pistachios

EQUIPMENT:

Parchment paper

TIME-SAVING TIP

You can find packaged roasted and peeled chestnuts in most grocery stores, often located in the kosher section. You can also find diced butternut squash in the produce section of your local grocery store.

Preheat the oven to 400°F. Line a large baking sheet with parchment paper.

Prepare the squash: Combine the squash, olive oil, and salt in a large bowl. Mix well so the squash is well coated. Arrange the squash on the lined baking sheet in a single layer and bake for 30 minutes.

Remove the squash from the oven, sprinkle with the brown sugar, and return the squash to the oven for an additional 15 minutes, or until caramelized. Set aside.

While the squash cooks, prepare the onions: Heat the olive oil in a large, deep, nonstick skillet. Add the sliced onions and salt and cook over medium-high heat for 5 to 7 minutes, or until translucent. Lower the heat to medium-low and continue to cook for another 45 minutes, or until golden brown and caramelized. Add the brown sugar, mix well, and cook for another 5 minutes. Add the chestnuts and continue to cook for 5 to 7 minutes. Add the dried cherries and cooked squash and toss gently. Remove from the heat and set aside.

Prepare the couscous: Combine the couscous, salt, paprika, turmeric, and cumin in a large bowl. Add the vegetable oil and gently rub the couscous between your hands, until it is well coated with the oil and spices. Add the 2 cups of boiling water, cover, and let sit for 10 minutes, or until the water has been absorbed, then fluff the couscous with a fork.

Prepare the nut topping: Heat the vegetable oil in a large, nonstick skillet. Add the almonds and pistachios and cook over medium-low heat for 3 to 5 minutes, or until golden, stirring constantly to prevent the nuts from burning.

Before serving, spoon the couscous onto the middle of a large serving platter. Arrange the squash mixture around the couscous, and sprinkle the almonds and pistachios on top and around the dish. Serve warm.

israeli couscous with sweet potato and delicata squash

Israeli couscous is a type of pasta that is shaped into tiny balls. It's also toasted, which gives it a slight nutty flavor. Our mom prepares it with lots of caramelized onions and chickpeas, and adds big chunks of cheese right at the end, so the cheese just starts to melt. Our dairy-free version adds sweet potato and delicata squash, adding a touch of sweetness and creaminess to the dish. Additionally, we sauté the pasta with spices before it cooks, to infuse some flavor and help keep it from sticking together. All in all, a comforting, warming, hearty dish!

Store in the refrigerator for up to four days. We do not recommend freezing this.

Prep time: 10 minutes
Cook time: 25 minutes
Makes 6 servings

INGREDIENTS:

2 tablespoons plus 2 teaspoons extra-virgin olive oil

1½ cups uncooked Israeli couscous

½ teaspoon ground turmeric

½ teaspoon smoked paprika

½ teaspoon garlic powder

2 cups boiling water

¾ to 1 teaspoon salt, to taste

1 medium-size red onion, sliced thinly

3 tablespoons balsamic vinegar

1 delicata squash, seeded, peeled, and diced

1 sweet potato, peeled and diced

1 (15-ounce) can chickpeas, drained and rinsed

Chopped fresh parsley, for garnish

Heat 2 teaspoons of the olive oil in a medium-size saucepan. Add the couscous, turmeric, smoked paprika, and garlic powder and cook over medium heat for 2 minutes, stirring constantly. Add the boiling water and ½ teaspoon of the salt and stir well. Bring to a boil, lower the heat to low, and simmer, covered, for 8 to 10 minutes, or until all the water has been absorbed and the couscous is tender. Remove from the heat and set aside.

Heat the remaining 2 tablespoons of olive oil in a large, deep skillet with a lid. Add the sliced onion and cook over medium heat for 2 minutes, stirring often, or until the onion starts to brown. Add the vinegar and continue to cook for 1 minute.

Add the squash, sweet potato, and the remaining ¼ to ½ teaspoon of salt, to taste, toss well, and cook for 5 minutes.

Add 3 tablespoons of water and the chickpeas, cover the skillet, and cook for 7 to 8 more minutes, tossing occasionally, or until the squash and the sweet potatoes are tender but still have a little bit of a bite to them.

Combine the couscous and sweet potato mixture in a large bowl and toss gently until well combined. Sprinkle the parsley on top and serve warm.

caramelized baby okra in tomato and pomegranate molasses sauce

We love cooking with baby okra because it doesn't release the off-putting gummy substance when it's cooked. Frozen baby okra can be found in Middle Eastern grocery stores and often in the kosher frozen section of conventional supermarkets. (You can use large okra if you like; just increase the amount to a pound and a half.)

The thick, rich sauce has a wonderful balance of sweetness and acidity, and is best served over plain rice (such as Lebanese White Rice with Vermicelli, page 144) or quinoa. If you prefer a thinner sauce, add a bit of hot water and stir it well.

Prep time: 5 minutes
Cook time: 1 hour 10 minutes
Makes 4 servings

INGREDIENTS:

2 tablespoons olive oil

¼ cup tomato paste

14 ounces frozen baby okra

4 garlic cloves, sliced

½ teaspoon salt

½ teaspoon baharat or ground allspice

½ teaspoon Aleppo pepper

3 cups canned crushed tomatoes

⅓ cup pomegranate molasses

Heat the oil in a large saucepan. Add the tomato paste and cook over medium-high heat for 3 to 4 minutes, stirring constantly.

Add the okra, garlic, salt, baharat, and Aleppo pepper, lower the heat to medium, and cook for 10 minutes, stirring often.

Add 1 cup of water, stir well, and continue to cook for another 10 minutes.

Add the crushed tomatoes and pomegranate molasses, lower the heat to low, and simmer, covered, for 40 minutes.

Serve warm with Lebanese White Rice with Vermicelli (page 144).

slow cooker sweet and savory moroccan-style tofu

This is a meatless version of our mom's sweet-and-sour Moroccan chicken. Filled with warm, smoky spices and with a slight sweetness coming from the dried fruit, every bit of this stew explodes with flavor. All you need is about fifteen minutes to prepare it, and let the slow cooker do all the work! Start the cooker before going to bed at night or going to work in the morning, and you'll have a delicious, balanced meal ready for dinner. Serve with plain couscous, quinoa, or Lebanese White Rice with Vermicelli (page 144).

This dish can be stored in the refrigerator for up to four days, and can be frozen for up to two months.

Prep time: 10 minutes
Cook time: 8 hours 5 minutes
Makes 6 servings

INGREDIENTS:

1 tablespoon smoked paprika

1 tablespoon garlic powder

1 tablespoon onion powder

2 teaspoons ground cumin

2 teaspoons ground turmeric

1 teaspoon salt

½ teaspoon freshly ground black pepper

16 ounces extra-firm tofu, cut into ½-inch dice

2 tablespoons extra-virgin olive oil

1 (15-ounce) can chickpeas, drained and rinsed

3 carrots, sliced

2 shallots, diced

15 pitted prunes, roughly chopped

15 dried apricots, roughly chopped

½ cup raisins

3 cups vegetable broth or water

2 cups freshly squeezed orange juice

½ cup balsamic vinegar

¼ cup freshly squeezed lemon juice

Sliced toasted almonds, for garnish (optional)

EQUIPMENT:

6-quart slow cooker

Combine the smoked paprika, garlic powder, onion powder, cumin, turmeric, salt, and black pepper in a small bowl and mix well. Set aside.

Combine the diced tofu with 1 tablespoon of the olive oil in a large bowl and mix well, using your hands. Add half of the spice mixture and mix again so the tofu is well coated.

Heat a large, nonstick skillet over medium heat. Add the tofu and cook for 3 to 4 minutes, stirring often, or until it starts to brown slightly.

Spread the remaining tablespoon of olive oil on the bottom of a 6-quart slow cooker. Add the cooked tofu and the remaining ingredients, except the almonds. Add the remaining spice mixture and stir well. Cook on HIGH for 8 hours. Garnish with sliced almonds before serving.

NO SLOW COOKER? NO PROBLEM;
HERE ARE STOVETOP INSTRUCTIONS:

Prepare the spices and cook the tofu as noted above.

Heat the remaining tablespoon of olive oil in a large soup pot. Add the carrots and shallots and cook over medium heat for 3 to 4 minutes, or until the shallots are translucent, stirring often. Add the balsamic vinegar and cook for an additional 4 minutes.

Add the prunes, apricots, raisins, broth or water, orange and lemon juice, and the remaining spice mixture. Cook over medium-high heat for 5 to 7 minutes, stirring occasionally.

Add the cooked tofu and chickpeas, lower the heat to low, and simmer for 30 minutes.

roasted cauliflower
with green tahini

This is our take on a traditional Israeli dish that is made with fried cauliflower and topped with tahini and pine nuts. Instead of frying, we have roasted the cauliflower head whole to accentuate its sweetness and for a unique presentation. The tahini blended with herbs adds some freshness and a beautiful color.

This dish pairs wonderfully with Cumin Jasmine Rice with Almonds, Walnuts, and Cashews (page 152) or Fava Bean and Fried Artichoke Basmati Rice (page 156).

Prep time: 10 minutes
Cook time: 55 minutes
Makes 4 to 6 servings

INGREDIENTS:

2 small cauliflower heads, leaves and
    stem removed

2 tablespoons extra-virgin olive oil

½ teaspoon salt

¼ teaspoon freshly ground black
    pepper

GREEN TAHINI SAUCE:

1 cup loosely packed fresh parsley

1 cup loosely packed fresh cilantro

¼ cup loosely packed fresh dill

⅓ cup plus 1 tablespoon tahini

⅓ cup freshly squeezed lemon juice

1 to 1½ teaspoons agave nectar or
    pure maple syrup

½ teaspoon salt

TOASTED PINE NUTS:

1 teaspoon extra-virgin olive oil

2 tablespoons raw pine nuts

Preheat the oven to 375°F. Line a large baking sheet with aluminum foil. Place the cauliflower heads on the lined baking sheet. Drizzle 1 tablespoon of the olive oil, ¼ teaspoon of the salt, and ⅛ teaspoon of the pepper on each head. Cover with aluminum foil and bake for 55 minutes, or until tender.

Prepare the green tahini sauce: Combine all the sauce ingredients plus ½ cup of water in a blender and blend until smooth. Refrigerate until you are ready to use it.

Toast the nuts: Heat the olive oil in a small skillet, add the pine nuts, and toast for 1 to 2 minutes, stirring constantly, or until golden.

Place the warm cauliflower on a serving platter, and top with green tahini and toasted pine nuts.

tempeh-stuffed zucchini
in mint tomato sauce

As noted in the pantry section, tempeh has a great meaty texture and not a very strong taste, so it pretty much absorbs the taste of the ingredients it is cooked with. Here, it's paired with mint and tomato, flavors often paired in Middle Eastern cooking. It's bright and fresh, and although it might seem a little unusual, it's absolutely delicious and worth a try!

The filling and sauce for this dish can be prepared two to three days ahead of time, and refrigerated separately until they are ready to be used. Serve it with Nutty Green Rice (page 148) or with a side of plain quinoa or couscous.

Prep time: 35 minutes (includes soaking time)
Cook time: 1 hour 10 minutes
Makes 4 servings

INGREDIENTS:

8 ounces tempeh, crumbled

2 cups boiling water

2 large zucchini, skin on, thoroughly washed, cut into 2-inch lengths

2 large yellow summer squash, skin on, thoroughly washed, cut into 2-inch lengths

1 tablespoon extra-virgin olive oil

¼ teaspoon salt

1 garlic clove, crushed

½ teaspoon onion powder

⅛ teaspoon freshly ground black pepper

¼ cup chopped walnuts

1 tablespoon pomegranate molasses (see page 132 for homemade)

MINT TOMATO SAUCE:

1 tablespoon extra-virgin olive oil

1 clove garlic, minced

1 (28-ounce) can crushed tomatoes

½ teaspoon onion powder

¼ teaspoon salt

⅛ teaspoon freshly ground black pepper

2 tablespoons freshly squeezed lemon juice

6 large mint leaves, chopped

Place the crumbled tempeh in a heatproof bowl. Pour the boiling water over it, cover with a plate, and let sit for 20 minutes. Drain well and set aside.

In the meantime, scoop the flesh from the zucchini and summer squash, using a spoon or a melon baller, being careful not to poke a hole into the sides or bottom of the peel; you want the peel to remain intact. Set the hollowed squash cylinders aside; place the scooped flesh on a cutting board and roughly chop it.

Once the tempeh is ready, heat the olive oil in a large, nonstick skillet. Add the chopped zucchini and salt and cook over medium-high heat for 6 to 7 minutes, stirring often, or until it starts to soften.

Add the drained tempeh, garlic, onion powder, and pepper and continue to cook for 4 minutes.

Add the walnuts and pomegranate molasses and cook for 2 more minutes, stirring constantly. Remove from the heat and set aside.

Prepare the mint tomato sauce: Heat the olive oil in a large, deep skillet with a lid. Add the garlic and cook over medium heat for about 30 seconds, stirring constantly. Add the tomatoes, onion powder, salt, and pepper. Stir well and continue to cook, covered, for 6 to 7 minutes (it's important to cover the skillet to prevent the sauce from splashing).

Add the lemon juice and mint, stir well, and cook, covered, for another 3 minutes. Pour the sauce into a 9 by 13-inch baking dish, covering the bottom of the dish.

Preheat the oven to 375°F.

Stuff each squash cylinder with about 1½ tablespoons of the tempeh mixture. Arrange the stuffed squash on the baking dish on top of the sauce. Cover the pan tightly with aluminum foil and bake for 45 minutes, until the squash is tender.

stuffed grape leaves with figs and blood orange

Making stuffed grape leaves from scratch is a pretty labor-intensive and time-consuming process. Thankfully, they can be found already prepared in cans or jars in most grocery stores. And even though they are traditionally stuffed with ground meat and rice, most of the ones we have found have a vegan rice and herb filling. Here, we rely on these conveniences to create a dish with a wonderful balance of sweetness from the dried fruit, tartness from the orange and pomegranate juices, and a touch of savory from the herbs in the filling.

Prep time: 10 minutes
Cook time: 1 hour 20 minutes
Makes 6 servings

INGREDIENTS:

- 30 canned stuffed grape leaves (about two 14-ounce cans)
- 1 cup small dried Black Mission figs, sliced in half
- 1 cup dried apricots
- 1 cup freshly squeezed blood orange juice or regular orange juice
- 1 cup pomegranate juice

Preheat the oven to 400°F.

Arrange half of the stuffed grape leaves on the bottom of a 7 by 11-inch baking dish. Place the figs on top, then the remaining stuffed grape leaves, and finally the apricots.

Pour the orange and pomegranate juice over the grape leaves, cover the baking dish tightly with aluminum foil, and bake for 1 hour.

Lower the oven temperature to 350°F, uncover, and bake for 20 more minutes.

181

the main event

stuffed tomatoes on a bed of zesty carrots

Summer, when tomatoes are abundant and full of flavor, is the perfect time for this tasty main dish. Stuffed vegetables are staples in Middle Eastern cuisine. While traditionally tomatoes are stuffed with a combination of rice and meat, our mom invented this meat-free version as more and more members of our family became vegetarian. It's important that you use a 9 by 13-inch baking dish with high sides, so the tomatoes don't come to the top, to prevent the juices from overflowing while they cook. Place the baking dish on a baking sheet, as noted in the instructions, to catch any drips.

Prep time: 15 minutes
Cook time: 2 hours 15 minutes
Makes 6 to 8 servings

INGREDIENTS:

1 teaspoon baharat or ground allspice

1 teaspoon ground cinnamon

1 tablespoon extra-virgin olive oil

12 medium-size tomatoes (all similar in size)

3 to 4 medium-size carrots, peeled and thinly cut lengthwise

FILLING:

1 cup uncooked white rice, preferably jasmine

1 tablespoon sumac

1¾ teaspoons salt

1 cup canned chickpeas, drained, rinsed, and slightly mashed

¼ cup olive oil

1 cup chopped fresh parsley

¼ cup pomegranate molasses (see page 132 for homemade)

TOPPING:

¾ cup pomegranate molasses (see page 132 for homemade)

2 tablespoons freshly squeezed lemon juice

¼ teaspoon salt

Combine the baharat and cinnamon in a small bowl and set aside.

Preheat the oven to 375°F. Coat the bottom of a 9 by 13-inch baking dish with the olive oil.

Cut off the tops of the tomatoes (do not discard) and, with a small spoon, carefully scoop out the flesh onto a cutting board, being careful not to poke a hole through the skin. Roughly chop the tomato flesh and place in a small bowl.

Prepare the filling: Combine the rice, sumac, 1½ teaspoons of the salt, 1 teaspoon of the baharat mixture, the chickpeas, 2 tablespoons of the olive oil, the parsley, and the pomegranate molasses in a medium-size bowl and mix well.

Fill the tomatoes about three-quarters full with the rice filling (the rice will need room to expand). Arrange the tomatoes in a single layer in the prepared baking dish, and top each with its reserved top. Wedge the carrots tightly in between the tomatoes. Drizzle with the remaining 2 tablespoons of olive oil. Sprinkle with the remaining ¼ teaspoon salt and the remaining teaspoon of the baharat mixture.

Fill the baking dish about three-quarters full with warm water, cover tightly with aluminum foil, place on top of a baking sheet, and bake for 1 hour.

Remove the baking dish from the oven, remove the foil, and pour the pomegranate molasses and lemon juice over the top. Arrange the reserved chopped tomato flesh on top and sprinkle with ¼ teaspoon of salt. Return the baking dish to the oven for 1 hour 15 minutes, or until the tomatoes are dark red.

TIME-SAVING TIP

Tomatoes can be stuffed and refrigerated up to two days ahead of time, to be cooked later.

stuffed onions

Of all the stuffed vegetables we make, onions are the ones that get the most requests by our family and friends. There's something about the combination of the pomegranate molasses, lemon juice, baharat, and cinnamon that, added to the natural sweetness of the onions, makes for an absolutely scrumptious and unique dish.

The process of stuffing the onion layers might sound difficult and time consuming, but it actually isn't. Because the layers naturally curl after the onions are boiled, they pretty much do all the work for you! Make sure to use large, sweet onions for this recipe. Avoid rinsing the fine bulgur wheat in a colander; the grains are too fine and they will fall through. Instead, fill a large bowl with water, add the bulgur, stir a few times with your hand, and carefully pour out the water.

Store the stuffed onions in the refrigerator for up to four days.

Prep time: 30 minutes
Cook time: 2 hours
Makes 6 servings

INGREDIENTS:

4 very large sweet onions

1 cup fine bulgur wheat, rinsed (see headnote)

½ cup walnuts, chopped

½ cup chopped fresh parsley

½ cup pomegranate molasses (see page 132 for homemade)

6 tablespoons neutral-flavor oil (such as sunflower, avocado, or grapeseed)

1 teaspoon salt

⅛ teaspoon freshly ground black pepper

½ teaspoon ground cinnamon

2 cups warm water

2 tablespoons freshly squeezed lemon juice

2 tablespoons sugar

¼ cup pomegranate seeds, for garnish (optional)

Fill a large soup pot with water and bring it to a boil.

In the meantime, using a sharp knife, remove the skin from the onions: make a vertical slit on each onion, about halfway down.

Place the onions in the boiling water and cook for 50 minutes, or until tender.

Carefully remove the onions from the water and place them in a large bowl. Let cool until safe to handle with your hands, but don't rinse them with cold water (you want the onions to keep cooking while they cool).

In the meantime, prepare the filling: Combine the rinsed bulgur wheat, chopped walnuts, parsley, ¼ cup of the pomegranate molasses, 2 tablespoons of the oil, ½ teaspoon of the salt, and the pepper in a large bowl and mix well.

Preheat the oven to 400°F. Coat the bottom of a 2-inch deep, 9 by 13-inch baking dish with 2 tablespoons of the oil.

Once the onions have cooled, very carefully separate each layer (the two or three outer layers of the onions will be larger, so they should be cut in half vertically).

Place a tablespoon of filling in the middle of each onion layer and roll it tightly.

Arrange the stuffed onions tightly on the prepared baking dish. Drizzle the remaining 2 tablespoons of oil on top and sprinkle with the remaining ½ teaspoon of salt and the cinnamon. Bake, uncovered, for 20 minutes.

Remove the baking dish from the oven. Add 2 cups of warm water, cover with aluminum foil, and return the dish to the oven for another 20 minutes.

Remove the dish from the oven again, drizzle with the remaining ¼ cup of pomegranate molasses and the lemon juice, and sprinkle the sugar on top. Return the dish to the oven and bake, uncovered, for 30 to 40 minutes, or until the onions are caramelized. Serve warm, garnished with pomegranate seeds, if desired.

sweet and savory quinoa-stuffed eggplant

We have simplified the laborious process of stuffing eggplant, and the long cooking time that comes along with it, by cooking the eggplant and filling separately. The creamy eggplant is topped with hearty quinoa mixed with meaty mushrooms, salty olives, and sweet sun-dried tomatoes. This dish can be served as a weeknight meal or as a great entrée on your holiday table. We love to serve it with a drizzle of Silan Tahini Dressing (page 136) on top.

Prep time: 20 minutes
Cook time: 45 minutes
Makes 4 servings

INGREDIENTS:

2 large eggplants, cut in half lengthwise, skin on

¼ cup plus 2 teaspoons extra-virgin olive oil

1¼ teaspoons salt

8 ounces baby bella mushrooms, chopped

⅛ teaspoon freshly ground black pepper

2 cups cooked quinoa

½ cup chopped fresh parsley or cilantro

6 kalamata olives, pitted and roughly chopped

6 black cured olives, pitted and roughly chopped

2 tablespoons za'atar

2 tablespoons sun-dried tomatoes packed in oil, chopped

1 teaspoon Aleppo pepper

½ cup pomegranate seeds

Silan Tahini Dressing (page 136; optional)

Preheat the oven to 400°F. Line a large baking sheet with parchment paper or aluminum foil. Place the eggplant halves, skin side down, on the baking sheet. Use a sharp knife to score the flesh with a diamond pattern, making sure not to cut so deeply as to poke holes in the skin. Brush 1 tablespoon of the olive oil and sprinkle ¼ teaspoon of the salt on each half. Bake for 30 minutes.

In the meantime, heat the remaining 2 teaspoons of the olive oil in a large skillet. Add the mushrooms, the remaining ¼ teaspoon of the salt, and the black pepper and cook over high heat for 3 to 4 minutes, or until all the water has evaporated.

Combine the quinoa, cooked mushrooms, parsley, olives, za'atar, sun-dried tomatoes, and Aleppo pepper in a large bowl and mix well.

Remove the eggplant from the oven, without turning it off. Spread one quarter of the quinoa mixture on top of each eggplant half, return the baking sheet to the oven, and bake for 15 minutes.

Before serving, top with pomegranate seeds and Silan Tahini Dressing.

mushroom-stuffed potato cradles

If you're familiar with Lebanese cuisine (and Middle Eastern in general), you may have noticed that it's big on stuffing things: vegetables, sweet and savory doughs, leaves . . . you name it, we find a stuffing for it. The one vegetable we have never seen stuffed, however, are potatoes. That is, until now! Creamy, buttery Yukon gold potatoes are stuffed with meaty mushrooms and lots of garlic, and cooked over a rich tomato sauce until tender.

Prep time: 25 minutes
Cook time: 1 hour 30 minutes
Makes 4 to 6 servings

INGREDIENTS:

12 medium-size organic Yukon gold potatoes (similar in shape and size), thoroughly scrubbed and washed

2 tablespoons extra-virgin olive oil

16 ounces baby bella mushrooms, chopped in a food processor

8 garlic cloves, minced

1 to 1¼ teaspoons salt

⅛ teaspoon freshly ground black pepper

½ cup chopped fresh cilantro, plus ¼ cup for garnish

3 shallots, chopped

2 tablespoons tomato paste

1 cup finely grated carrot

1 (28-ounce can) crushed tomatoes

1 tablespoon Good-on-Everything Spice Mix (page 131)

2 tablespoons pomegranate molasses (see page 132 for homemade)

Cut the potatoes in half. Using a melon baller or a spoon, scoop out the center of the potatoes, leaving about a ⅓-inch rim (place both the potatoes and the scooped-out centers in two separate bowls of cold water, and reserve the centers for future use).

Heat 1 tablespoon of the olive oil in a large, deep, nonstick skillet with a lid. Add the chopped mushrooms, half of the minced garlic, ½ teaspoon of the salt, and the pepper. Cook over high heat for 8 to 10 minutes, stirring often, or until the mushrooms are dry.

Lower the heat to medium, add the cilantro, and cook for another 2 minutes. Transfer the mushrooms to a bowl and set aside.

Using the same skillet, heat the remaining tablespoon of olive oil. Add the shallots, remaining minced garlic, and ¼ teaspoon of the salt. Cook over medium heat for about 5 minutes, or until the shallots are translucent, stirring often.

Add the tomato paste and the grated carrot to the skillet. Cook for 5 minutes, stirring frequently. Add the crushed tomatoes, spice mixture, pomegranate molasses, and ¼ cup of water and cook, covered, over medium-high heat for 10 minutes.

In the meantime, sprinkle the potatoes with ¼ to ½ teaspoon of salt. Fill each potato half with about 1 tablespoon of the cooked mushrooms and arrange them in the sauté pan over the tomato sauce, cut side up. Bring to a boil, cover the skillet, lower the heat to low, and simmer for 1 hour, or until the potatoes are tender. Garnish with chopped fresh cilantro. Serve warm.

hearty peas and carrots with beet and chickpea meatless meatballs

This recipe is our take on a peas, carrots, and meatball dish Mami makes often on Friday nights. The combination of baharat and cinnamon makes for a unique flavor profile that blends beautifully with the sweetness of the peas and carrots. The beet and chickpea meatballs are so hearty and flavorful, the meat is not at all missed.

Prep time: 30 minutes (includes refrigeration time)
Cook time: 2 hours 30 minutes (1 hour 30 minutes if using store-bought roasted beets)
Makes 6 servings

INGREDIENTS:

MEATBALLS:

1 (15-ounce) can chickpeas, drained and rinsed

¾ cup chopped fresh cilantro

2 medium-size roasted beets (page 78), or store-bought cooked beets

2 tablespoons freshly squeezed lemon juice

1 teaspoon ground turmeric

1 teaspoon Aleppo pepper

½ teaspoon ground cumin

½ teaspoon salt

1 cup flour (any kind will work here)

¼ cup neutral-flavor oil (such as sunflower, avocado, or grapeseed), for panfrying

PEAS AND CARROTS:

2 tablespoons extra-virgin olive oil

1 medium-size onion, diced

2 pounds frozen peas (about 6 cups)

2 cups peeled, small-diced carrot

½ to ¾ teaspoon salt

¾ teaspoon baharat or ground allspice

½ teaspoon ground cinnamon

TIME-SAVING TIP

Buy a frozen peas and carrot mix instead of using fresh carrots.

Place the chickpeas in a food processor and pulse until they're coarsely chopped. Transfer to a large bowl, add the chopped cilantro, and set aside.

Place the beets, lemon juice, turmeric, Aleppo pepper, cumin, and salt in the food processor and process until smooth. Add the mixture to the chopped chickpeas mixture, add the flour, and mix well. Let it sit in the refrigerator for 20 minutes.

Working with 1½ tablespoons at a time, form about two dozen meatballs (we like using a small ice-cream scoop, so they're all equal in size).

Heat the oil in a small saucepan. Add two to three meatballs at a time and cook them over medium-high heat, 4 to 5 minutes per side, or until they start to brown (make sure the oil doesn't get too hot, because the sugar in the beets will burn easily). Set aside.

> **TIP**
>
> If you prefer not to panfry them, the meatballs can also be baked in the oven. Generously grease a mini muffin pan, scoop about 1½ tablespoons of the mixture into each well, and bake at 400°F for 20 to 25 minutes.

Prepare the peas and carrots: Heat the olive oil in a large, deep skillet with a lid. Add the onion and cook over medium-high heat for 5 minutes, or until translucent.

Add the peas, carrots, salt, baharat, and cinnamon and stir well. Cover the skillet, lower the heat to low, and cook for 45 minutes, or until the peas and carrots are tender and infused with the spices. Gently add the meatballs and continue to cook for another 15 minutes.

Serve warm with Cumin Jasmine Rice with Almonds, Walnuts, and Cashews (page 152).

quinoa harissa meatless meatballs with artichokes in aromatic turmeric broth

Harissa is a North African condiment, made with hot chiles, garlic, olive oil, and an array of warm, aromatic spices. It infuses these meatless meatballs with a wonderful, intense flavor. The turmeric broth is fragrant, warm, and comforting, with earthy, slightly gingery flavors.

In this recipe, it's the vital wheat gluten that gives a meaty consistency, and helps the meatballs keep their shape.

Prep time: 1 hour (includes refrigeration time)
Cook time: 1 hour 30 minutes
Makes 6 servings

INGREDIENTS:

MEATBALLS:

Cooking spray

⅔ cup cooked quinoa

½ cup chopped walnuts

⅓ cup vital wheat gluten

¼ cup finely chopped fresh cilantro

2 garlic cloves, roughly chopped

3 tablespoons harissa

2 tablespoons all-purpose flour

1 tablespoon extra-virgin olive oil

1 teaspoon aniseeds

1 teaspoon ground coriander

1 teaspoon paprika

½ teaspoon salt

BROTH:

3 medium-size Yukon gold potatoes, peeled and cut into 8 pieces each

14 ounces frozen artichoke hearts, thawed, or use jarred or canned, well drained

1¼ teaspoons salt

1 teaspoon ground turmeric

⅛ teaspoon freshly ground black pepper

⅓ cup freshly squeezed lemon juice

½ cup chopped fresh parsley (optional)

Prepare the meatballs: Preheat the oven to 350°F. Generously coat a 12-well mini muffin tin with cooking spray. Place the cooked quinoa in a large bowl and set aside. Combine the walnuts, gluten, cilantro, garlic, harissa, flour, olive oil, aniseeds, coriander, paprika, and salt in a food processor and pulse until well combined. Add the mixture to the cooked quinoa and mix well, using your hands, to form a dough (note that it will be sticky; if it's too hard to handle, flour your hands lightly). Working with approximately 1½ tablespoons of dough at a time, form twelve balls and place them in the prepared muffin tin (we like using a small ice-cream scoop, so they're all equal in size). Bake for 45 minutes, or until the meatballs are firm.

Prepare the broth: Bring 4 cups of water to a boil in a large, deep skillet with a lid over medium-high heat. Add the potatoes, artichokes, salt, turmeric, and pepper. Cover and cook for 20 minutes, until the potatoes and artichokes are tender. Lower the heat to low and add the lemon juice, parsley, and meatballs. Cover and simmer for 15 minutes.

TIP

The meatball mixture can be prepared one to two days ahead, and kept covered in the refrigerator until it's ready to be used. It also makes a great veggie burger; just make larger patties!

Serve warm with Lebanese White Rice with Vermicelli (page 144).

bulgur wheat pie (*kibbeh*)

Kibbeh is probably one of the most popular Middle Eastern delicacies. They're little oval pockets of bulgur wheat dough, stuffed with ground meat, pine nuts, and spices, and fried until crispy. Kibbeh can also be made into a pie and baked in the oven, which is the way our mom makes it most often. They are both served with tahini sauce (Basic Tahini Sauce, page 133).

Our version uses chopped baby bella mushrooms and chopped pecans, for a meaty texture. The bulgur wheat dough is traditionally made with ground meat to act as a binder and add some moisture; we use canned pumpkin instead.

The kibbeh (raw or baked) can be frozen for up to two months.

Prep time: 40 minutes
Cook time: 1 hour
Makes 4 to 6 servings

INGREDIENTS:

DOUGH:

1 cup fine (#1) bulgur wheat

1 cup boiling water

1 cup canned pure pumpkin puree

⅓ cup all-purpose flour

3 tablespoons extra-virgin olive oil

2 teaspoons sweet paprika

1 teaspoon salt

½ teaspoon ground cumin

½ teaspoon ground turmeric

FILLING:

¼ teaspoon baharat or allspice

¼ teaspoon cinnamon

2 pounds baby bella mushrooms, sliced

2 tablespoons extra-virgin olive oil

¼ teaspoon salt

½ cup chopped toasted pecans

3 tablespoons pomegranate molasses
(see page 132 for homemade)

2 tablespoons neutral-flavor oil (such as
sunflower, avocado, or grapeseed)

4 tablespoons pine nuts

Combine the bulgur wheat and boiling water in a large, heatproof bowl. Cover with a large plate and let sit for 20 minutes, or until all the water has been absorbed. If there is any excess water, squeeze it out with your hands.

Add the pumpkin, flour, olive oil, paprika, salt, cumin, and turmeric. Mix well, using your hands, until it comes together to form a dough. Set aside.

Prepare the filling: Finely chop the sliced mushrooms in a food processor (we recommend doing this in two batches, so they chop evenly).

Heat the olive oil in a large skillet. Add the mushrooms and cook over high heat for 3 minutes, or until they start to release water. Add the salt, baharat, and cinnamon and continue to cook for another 5 to 7 minutes, or until the water has evaporated, stirring constantly.

Lower the heat to low, add the pecans, 3 tablespoons of the pine nuts, and pomegranate molasses, and cook for 3 to 4 minutes. Remove from the heat and set aside.

Meanwhile, preheat the oven to 375°F. Spread 1 tablespoon of the neutral-flavor oil on the bottom of an 9.5-inch pie dish.

Set aside 2 cups of the bulgur wheat dough. Press the remaining dough onto the bottom of the pie dish and prick all over with a fork. Spread the mushroom filling evenly on top.

Divide the 2 cups of reserved dough into eight to ten balls. Gently flatten each with your hands and place on top of the filling, until it's completely covered. Score the dough to make a diamond pattern. Arrange the remaining tablespoon of pine nuts in the middle of each diamond. Drizzle the remaining tablespoon of neutral-flavor oil on top and bake for 55 minutes, or until golden brown. Serve with Basic Tahini Sauce (page 133).

panfried herbed falafel patties

This may be a healthier twist on the classic, but it is still crispy and delicious! We shape our made-from-scratch falafel into patties, then panfry them to make them a little bit lighter. Dried (not canned) chickpeas and spices give these patties the characteristic falafel flavor; fresh cilantro and parsley add freshness and flavor. They can be served in a sandwich with pita bread, or in a platter. Basic Tahini Sauce (page 133) and Spicy Israeli Salsa (page 62) are a must! Other toppings we love are hummus, shredded purple cabbage, pickles, and hot sauce.

   The cooked patties can be frozen for up to one month.

Prep time: 10 minutes (does not include soaking time)
Cook time: 20 minutes
Makes 18 to 20 patties

INGREDIENTS:

1 cup dried chickpeas, soaked overnight in 4 cups water plus 1 teaspoon baking soda

1¼ cups chopped fresh parsley

1¼ cups chopped fresh cilantro

¼ cup chickpea flour

1 teaspoon ground coriander

1 teaspoon lemon zest

1 teaspoon salt

½ teaspoon ground cumin

½ teaspoon freshly ground black pepper

½ teaspoon Aleppo pepper

½ teaspoon ground turmeric

½ teaspoon garlic powder

¼ teaspoon ground allspice

⅛ teaspoon ground cardamom

2 tablespoons extra-virgin olive oil

¼ cup neutral-flavor oil (such as sunflower, grapeseed, or avocado), for panfrying

TOPPINGS:

Basic Tahini Sauce (page 133)

Spicy Israeli Salsa (page 62)

Shredded purple cabbage

Line a large plate with parchment or waxed paper. Set aside.

Combine all the ingredients, except the olive and neutral oil, in a food processor.

Pulse a few times, until all the ingredients are well combined and the mixture is slightly coarse. Add the olive oil and pulse a few more times, until well incorporated.

Working with 1½ tablespoons of mixture at a time, form a ball and flatten it slightly with the palm of your hand. Place the patties on the lined plate.

Heat the neutral oil in a medium-size skillet over medium heat. Add two or three falafel patties and cook for 5 minutes per side, or until crispy. Drain on paper towels. Repeat the process with the remaining patties.

Serve topped with tahini sauce, Israeli salsa, shredded purple cabbage, and pita bread.

cannellini bean and meatless sausage stew

This hearty stew is exactly what you need to warm up during the cold winter months. The smoky paprika, along with a hint of heat from the chili powder, gives the broth a complex, intense flavor you'll want to soak up with a crunchy piece of bread. The potatoes, beans, and meatless sausage make it a well-rounded, one-pot meal that will keep you satisfied for hours.

Store it in the refrigerator for up to four days. We don't recommend freezing this.

Prep time: 10 minutes
Cook time: 55 minutes
Makes 4 to 6 servings

INGREDIENTS:

2 tablespoons extra-virgin olive oil

1 heaping tablespoon smoked paprika

2 teaspoons chili powder

2 meatless sausages, cut into ½-inch slices

3 garlic cloves, sliced

1 teaspoon onion powder

½ teaspoon salt

6 small red potatoes, thoroughly washed and scrubbed, then quartered

2 (15-ounce) cans cannellini beans, with their liquid

Combine the olive oil, smoked paprika, and chili powder in a large soup pot over medium heat and cook for 1 minute, stirring

> TIP
>
> You can use your favorite kind of sausage for this dish, substitute diced, extra-firm tofu, or simply add another kind of bean (chickpeas work wonderfully here).

constantly, or until fragrant. Add the sausage and continue to cook for 2 minutes, or until it starts to brown.

Add the garlic and cook for 1 minute, stirring constantly so it doesn't burn. Add 3 cups of water and the onion powder, salt, potatoes, and beans with their liquid.

Bring to a boil, lower the heat to low, and simmer, covered, for 20 minutes, or until the potatoes are tender.

Remove the lid, increase the heat to medium, and cook for 30 more minutes, stirring occasionally, until some of the water has evaporated and the stew has thickened slightly.

Serve warm with fresh crusty bread.

ZA'ATAR MANAISH

9

fresh from the oven

Homemade savory pastries, crackers, and breads are a long-standing tradition in Middle Eastern cooking—and they always have a place at our family's table. Our grandmother always has *ka'ak* and coffee ready when we visit her in Tel Aviv. Our mom made challah rolls for us on Friday nights, and when we moved to the United States, we started experimenting with vegan versions and different flavors. From *manaish* (za'atar flatbread) to *bourekas* (savory stuffed pastries), we wanted to make sure we could enjoy plant-based versions of these classics. And now our own families have become so accustomed to eating homemade bread that they expect a new one every week!

savory sesame and nigella seed fingers (*ka'ak*)

As far as we can remember, our grandmother always had a fresh batch of *ka'ak* ready to serve her guests. This delicious Iraqi cracker is traditionally served with Turkish coffee but, trust us, they are good all by themselves. The nigella seeds add a slight oniony flavor; and the anise seeds, a fresh licorice taste. As a variation, you can add three tablespoons of za'atar to the dough, which makes these crackers herby, nutty, and slightly tangy.

Store them in an airtight container for up to a week or freeze for up to two months.

Prep time: 1 hour 30 minutes (includes rising time)
Cook time: 30 minutes
Makes 44 crackers

INGREDIENTS:

¾ cup extra-virgin olive oil, plus more for oiling bowl

2 tablespoons aniseeds

1 tablespoon nigella seeds

3 cups all-purpose flour, sifted

2 teaspoons active dry yeast

2 teaspoons sugar

1 teaspoon salt

¾ cup lukewarm water

½ cup unsweetened nondairy milk

½ to 1 cup sesame seeds, for garnish

EQUIPMENT:

Standing mixer with dough hook attachment

Parchment paper

TIP

These crackers freeze well once they are baked. They are great to have around, so we encourage you to make the whole recipe and freeze some for later use. Restore the crunch by warming them in a 200°F oven for 5 minutes.

Oil a large glass bowl and set aside.

Combine the aniseeds and nigella seeds with ⅓ cup of water in a small bowl. Set aside.

Combine the flour, yeast, sugar, and salt in a standing mixer bowl. Drain the seeds and add them to the bowl. Using the dough hook attachment, mix at low speed until well combined. Add the olive oil and water and mix until all the ingredients come together to form a dough, 1 to 2 minutes. Scrape down the sides and bottom of the bowl occasionally so all the flour is well incorporated.

Transfer the dough to the oiled glass bowl. Cover with a clean towel and let sit until the dough doubles in size, 45 to 60 minutes.

Line two large baking sheets with parchment paper. Once the dough has risen, divide the dough into quarters and roll each portion of dough into about eleven balls, for a total of forty-four dough balls. Roll each ball into 7½-inch-long logs and place on the lined baking sheets.

Brush each log with nondairy milk and sprinkle the sesame seeds on top, pressing gently so they stick to the dough. Cover the baking sheets with a clean towel and let the dough rest for 15 minutes.

In the meantime, preheat the oven to 400°F.

Bake each pan for 10 minutes, then rotate the pan, lower the oven temperature to 275°F, and bake for an additional 20 minutes, until the crackers start to brown lightly.

gluten-free falafel crackers

Made with chickpea flour and filled with warm spices, these crackers will make you think you're eating crunchy falafel bites! They are full of flavor, and nutritionally speaking, a lot healthier than most boxed crackers you'll find. They can be eaten plain, or with any of our "Appetite Teasers" dips or "Body Warmers." Store in an airtight container for up to five days.

Prep time: 15 minutes
Cook time: 15 minutes
Makes about 75 crackers, depending on the size

INGREDIENTS:

1 cup chickpea flour, plus more for dusting

2 tablespoons white sesame seeds

2 tablespoons black sesame seeds

1 teaspoon salt

1 teaspoon sweet paprika

½ teaspoon hot paprika, or to taste

¾ teaspoon ground cumin

¾ teaspoon ground coriander

½ teaspoon ground turmeric

¼ teaspoon ground allspice

⅛ teaspoon freshly ground black pepper

⅛ teaspoon ground cardamom

3 tablespoons extra-virgin olive oil

2 tablespoons tahini

EQUIPMENT:
Parchment paper

Preheat the oven to 375°F. Cut a piece of parchment paper large enough to fit a large baking sheet and flour it lightly. Set the prepared parchment aside.

Combine the flour, sesame seeds, salt, both paprikas, cumin, coriander, turmeric, allspice, pepper, and cardamom in a large bowl and mix well. Add ¼ cup of water, olive oil, and tahini. Mix well, using your hands, until it forms a soft dough.

Roll the dough into a rectangle about ¹⁄₁₆ inch thick on the parchment. Transfer it to the baking sheet. Using a pizza cutter or a sharp knife, score the dough into small squares. Bake for 13 to 14 minutes, or until golden brown. Remove from the oven and let cool completely.

GLUTEN-FREE FALAFEL CRACKERS

ZA'ATAR FLAX CRACKERS

za'atar flax crackers

These gluten-free, low-carb crackers take a little bit of time to bake, but are extremely easy to prepare. The most challenging part is flipping the cracker sheet onto the parchment paper, after it bakes for the first fifty minutes. But even if it breaks or cracks, it is completely fine, since it will be broken into pieces later on. For equal-size crackers, score the dough with a knife before placing it in the oven.

Serve these with any of the dips in the "Appetite Teasers" chapter. Store in an airtight container for up to five days.

Prep time: 25 minutes
Cook time: 1 hour 15 minutes
Makes about 35 crackers, depending on the size

INGREDIENTS:

½ cup whole flaxseeds

½ cup ground flaxseeds

3 tablespoons chia seeds

Cooking spray

3 tablespoons shelled raw sunflower seeds

3 tablespoons shelled raw pumpkin seeds

1 teaspoon salt

3 tablespoons za'atar

1 tablespoon pure maple syrup or silan (optional)

Neutral-flavor oil (such as sunflower, grapeseed, or avocado), for oiling hands

EQUIPMENT:

Parchment paper

Combine the whole flaxseeds, ground flaxseeds, chia seeds, and 1 cup of water in a large bowl and let soak for 15 to 20 minutes.

Preheat the oven to 300°F. Line an 11 by 17-inch baking sheet with parchment paper and coat it with cooking spray. Cut another piece of parchment to the same size as the other, and place it next to the lined baking sheet. Set aside.

Once the seeds are ready, add the sunflower and pumpkin seeds, salt, za'atar, and syrup. Mix well, using your hands.

Oil your hands slightly and spread the mixture on the lined baking sheet as evenly as possible. If you want to score the dough to have equal-size crackers, do so now.

Bake for 50 minutes.

Remove the baking sheet from the oven. Flip the cracker sheet over onto the prepared piece of parchment, place on the baking sheet again, and bake for another 15 minutes. Turn off the oven and let the pan sit inside for 10 minutes.

Remove the baking sheet from the oven and let the crackers cool completely. Break them into uneven pieces (see headnote).

za'atar manaish

Walk down the streets of the Shuk in Jerusalem and you'll find vendors all around selling *manaish*. This flatbread is often eaten for breakfast or as an afternoon snack, and is traditionally topped with za'atar or salty cheese.

Manaish can be frozen for up to two months, and reheated in a 300°F oven for five to seven minutes.

Prep time: 2 hours 45 minutes (includes rising time)
Cook time: 7 minutes per batch
Makes 6

INGREDIENTS:

½ cup extra-virgin olive oil

1½ teaspoons active dry yeast

¾ cup warm water

1 teaspoon sugar

2 cups bread flour, plus more for
    dusting (if mixing by hand)

½ cup spelt flour

1 teaspoon salt

TOPPING:

¼ cup plus 1 tablespoon za'atar

3 tablespoons extra-virgin olive oil

EQUIPMENT:

Standing mixer with dough hook
    attachment

Parchment paper

BY HAND METHOD:

Oil a large glass bowl with ¼ cup of the olive oil and set aside.

Combine the yeast, water, and sugar in a small bowl. Mix well and set aside.

TIME-SAVING TIP

If you don't have time to prepare the dough from scratch, you can use fresh store-bought pizza dough from the grocery store or your local pizza place.

Place both flours in a large bowl. Add the yeast and ¼ cup of the olive oil and mix well until the dough starts to come together. Transfer to a floured surface and knead the dough until smooth (the dough might be sticky).

Place in the oiled bowl, cover with a clean kitchen towel, and let rise for 2 hours, or until the dough doubles in size.

STANDING MIXER METHOD:

Combine the yeast, water, and sugar in the standing mixer bowl and mix well. Add ¼ cup of olive oil, both flours, and the salt. Using the dough hook attachment, knead on medium to high speed for about 5 minutes, until it forms a dough that pulls away from the sides of the bowl.

Cover the bowl with a clean kitchen towel and let rise for 2 hours, or until the dough doubles in size.

Once the dough has risen, divide it into six equal pieces and roll each into a smooth ball.

Place the dough balls on a tray, cover them with a clean kitchen towel, and let rise for 30 minutes.

In the meantime, prepare the topping: Mix the za'atar and 3 tablespoons of olive oil in a bowl. Set aside.

Preheat the oven to 500°F.

Cut three pieces of parchment paper, each big enough to fit a large baking sheet, and flour them lightly. Once the dough has risen for the second time, roll each ball into a 6½-inch circle on the parchment paper (two balls per piece of paper).

Spread the za'atar mixture over the dough, using the back of a spoon. Place one of the pieces of parchment paper, with its *manaish*, on a large baking sheet. Bake for 7 minutes. Repeat twice more with the other rolled-out dough. Serve warm.

sweet challah rolls

While we were growing up, our mom used to make challah rolls for our Friday night dinners. Occasionally, she would surprise us by putting a big square of dark chocolate in some of the rolls—a real treat! We've been wanting to re-create our mom's challah for some time, but since baking (and especially bread making) is such an exact science, we didn't attempt to make vegan challah until recently. After a few tries, we came up with the perfect ratio of ingredients and substitutions. In this recipe, the mixture of milk and ground flax takes the place of the egg. It's important to sift the flour, so the dough turns out soft and smooth.

Store the rolls at room temperature for two to three days, or in the freezer for up to two months.

Prep time: 2 hours 45 minutes (includes rising time)
Cook time: 25 minutes
Makes 12 rolls

INGREDIENTS:

½ cup lukewarm water

1 tablespoon active dry yeast

2 tablespoons plus 2 teaspoons sugar

¼ cup plus 2 tablespoons coconut oil, melted, plus more for bowl

½ cup unsweetened nondairy milk

2 tablespoons ground flaxseeds

3 cups all-purpose flour, sifted, plus more for dusting

1 teaspoon salt

¼ cup pure maple syrup

Cooking spray

White and black sesame seeds, for sprinkling

EQUIPMENT:

Standing mixer with dough hook attachment

12-well muffin tin

Pastry brush

Combine the lukewarm water, yeast, and 2 teaspoons of the sugar in a small bowl and stir well. Set aside.

Oil a large glass bowl and set aside.

In a separate bowl, mix together the milk and ground flaxseeds. Set aside.

Combine the sifted flour, remaining 2 tablespoons of sugar, and salt in the bowl of a standing mixer fitted with a dough hook attachment. Add the yeast and flax mixtures, ¼ cup plus 1 tablespoon of the coconut oil, and the maple syrup. Mix the dough on medium speed for 3 to 5 minutes, making sure all the flour from the bottom of the bowl gets well incorporated. Transfer the dough to the oiled bowl, cover with a clean kitchen towel, and let rise for 2 hours, or until the dough doubles in size.

In the meantime, place the remaining tablespoon of melted coconut oil in a small bowl, and the sesame seeds in two separate bowls, and set them aside with the pastry brush until you are ready to use them.

Once the dough has risen, coat the wells of a 12-well muffin tin with cooking spray. Divide the dough into four equal portions, and divide each portion into three equal pieces, rolling them into balls on a floured surface (you should have a total of twelve dough balls).

Roll each ball into a log about 7½ inches long, and each log into a spiral bun shape. Place them in the prepared muffin tin, very gently brush with melted coconut oil, and sprinkle with the sesame seeds. Cover with a clean towel and let rise for 30 minutes.

Meanwhile, preheat the oven to 350°F. Bake the rolls for 25 minutes, or until golden brown.

za'atar and seed bread topped with dukkah

There is something special about baking bread that fills the house with a warm, inviting smell. For us, it's the ultimate comfort food! Making it at home might sound like a daunting task, but the process is surprisingly simple. Using a standing mixer will save you some muscle work, but if you don't have one, it can be prepared perfectly by hand.

Sweet cranberries, savory za'atar, and hearty seeds come together beautifully in this rustic-looking bread. Use it to soak the tomato sauce of our Chickpea and Pepper Shakshuka (page 20) or dip it into a good olive oil sprinkled with salt. It's also absolutely delicious toasted with a little coconut oil spread on top. The baked bread can be frozen for up to a month.

Prep time: 3 hours (includes rising time)
Cook time: 20 minutes
Makes 2 loaves

INGREDIENTS:

Neutral-flavor oil, for bowl

1¾ cups whole wheat pastry flour

1¼ cups white bread flour

½ cup spelt flour

¼ cup za'atar

⅓ cup dried cranberries

2 tablespoons sugar

2 tablespoons sunflower seeds

2 tablespoons pumpkin seeds

2 tablespoons shelled pistachios

1 tablespoon active dry yeast

1 tablespoon salt

1½ cups warm water

2 teaspoons Dukkah (page 130; optional)

EQUIPMENT:

Standing mixer with dough hook attachment

Parchment paper

> TIP
>
> If you don't have spelt flour on hand, you can increase the amount of whole wheat pastry flour and white bread flour by ¼ cup each.

STANDING MIXER METHOD:

Oil a large glass bowl and set aside.

Combine the flours, za'atar, cranberries, sugar, sunflower and pumpkin seeds, pistachios, yeast, and salt in the bowl of a standing mixer fitted with a dough hook attachment. Mix well, add the warm water, and mix on medium speed for 3 to 5 minutes, making sure all the flour from the bottom of the bowl gets well incorporated.

HANDMADE METHOD:

Combine the flours, za'atar, cranberries, sugar, sunflower and pumpkin seeds, pistachios, yeast, and salt in a large bowl and mix well. Add the warm water and work the mixture with your hands, making sure all the flour from the bottom of the bowl gets well incorporated. Knead the dough for 2 to 3 minutes.

Place the dough in the oiled bowl, cover with a clean kitchen towel, and let rise for 2 hours, or until doubled in size.

Line a baking sheet with parchment paper. Divide the dough in half, form each portion into a 7-inch loaf, and place both 3 inches apart on the lined baking sheet. Cover with a clean kitchen towel and let rise again for 1 hour, or until they almost double in size.

Meanwhile, preheat the oven to 450°F. Using a serrated knife, make one vertical cut and three horizontal ones on the top of each loaf. Gently brush the loaves with water and sprinkle with the *dukkah*, if using. Bake for 20 minutes, or until golden brown.

abuelita's savory bourekas

Of the many delicious treats our grandmother (Abuelita) makes, the one that remind us of her the most are her cheese *bourekas*. They're the absolute best we've ever had. Even our neighbors used to get all excited knowing she would be coming to visit, hoping she would bake a batch for them!

Our vegan version of these buttery, savory pastries are filled with homemade cashew "ricotta," a touch of nutritional yeast for cheeselike flavor, and pumpkin or squash puree, to add some moisture.

The *bourekas* can be frozen for up to a month.

Prep time: 50 minutes
Cook time: 30 minutes
Makes 12

INGREDIENTS:

FILLING:

2 cups boiling water

1 cup raw cashews

2 tablespoons nutritional yeast

2 teaspoons coconut oil

2 tablespoons freshly squeezed lemon juice (from 1 small lemon)

½ teaspoon salt

½ cup canned pure pumpkin or butternut squash puree

DOUGH:

1⅓ cups all-purpose flour, plus more for dusting

½ teaspoon baking powder

¼ teaspoon salt

½ cup coconut oil

3 to 5 tablespoons cold unsweetened nondairy milk

OPTIONAL GARNISH:

Melted coconut oil

Sesame seeds

EQUIPMENT:

Parchment paper

Combine the boiling water and cashews in a heatproof bowl and let soak for 30 minutes. Drain well and set aside.

In the meantime, prepare the dough: Combine the flour, baking powder, and salt in a food processor and pulse three or four times. Add the coconut oil and pulse a few more times, until the mixture resembles coarse cornmeal.

Add the milk (start with 3 tablespoons and add more if necessary) and continue to pulse until the dough starts to come together. Transfer the dough to a lightly floured surface and roll it into a ball. Let rest until the filling is ready.

Prepare the filling: Combine the soaked cashews, nutritional yeast, coconut oil, lemon juice, and salt in the food processor. Pulse until smooth. Transfer it to a bowl and fold in the pumpkin or butternut squash until well incorporated. Set aside.

Preheat the oven to 350°F. Line a large baking sheet with parchment paper.

Roll out the dough into a circle, about ⅛ inch thick, on a lightly floured surface. Using a drinking glass or cookie cutter, cut out as many 3½-inch rounds as you can. Reroll the dough and continue to cut rounds until you have used all the dough (you should end up with about twelve rounds).

Slightly stretch each round with your fingers and spoon about 1½ teaspoons of filling onto the center. Fold it to create a half-moon shape and seal the edges, using your fingers or a fork. Arrange the filled crescents on the lined baking sheet and bake for 27 to 30 minutes, or until golden brown.

As an optional garnish, you can lightly brush the *bourekas* with melted coconut oil and sprinkle sesame seeds on top.

CREAMY TAHINI CHEESECAKE
WITH PISTACHIO CRUST AND
FRESH POMEGRANATE

10

sweet endings

Growing up, our after-dinner dessert was always fruit. But at holidays, celebrations, or when we went out for dinner, we devoured our sweet treats! These desserts are wonderfully flavored with floral waters, pistachios, and tahini. Although floral waters may be new to you, they are fairly easy to find and add a light, fresh taste to some of these delicate treats. You'll also enjoy our nut-stuffed *maamoul* cookies, made with coconut oil instead of butter; our take on the classic black and white cookies, with rich tahini as a base and topped with crunchy sesame seeds; and a uniquely sweet candied spaghetti squash tart sprinkled with sugar and pine nuts.

tahini truffles

Chocolate and tahini are two of our favorite things in the world. And these rich, decadent truffles are the perfect way to enjoy them both together!

We like using a 2-teaspoon ice-cream scoop to make sure all the truffles are the same size. If you don't have one, use 2 teaspoons of chocolate mixture per truffle. Store them in the refrigerator in an airtight container for up to one week, or in the freezer for up to three months.

Prep time: 15 minutes
Makes 30 truffles

INGREDIENTS:

1 cup vegan chocolate chips

1 cup canned light coconut milk

½ cup tahini

2 tablespoons unsweetened cocoa powder

2 tablespoons toasted sesame seeds

OPTIONAL TOPPINGS:

Ground pistachios, toasted sesame seeds, black sesame seeds, shredded coconut, beet powder, unsweetened cocoa powder

TIP

Use your favorite toppings to roll the truffles! We love using beet powder to add a fun, bright color!

Place the chocolate chips in a large, heatproof glass bowl.

In a small saucepan, bring the coconut milk to a simmer over medium-low heat (make sure it does not come to a boil). Remove from the heat and pour over the chocolate chips. Stir until the chocolate has melted completely.

Whisk in the tahini and cocoa powder until well incorporated. Add the sesame seeds and mix well.

Cover the bowl with plastic wrap and refrigerate it for at least 4 hours or overnight, until the mixture has set.

Once the chocolate is ready, place your topping (or toppings) of choice in a small bowl or bowls. Working with about 2 teaspoons at a time (you can use a small ice-cream scoop or melon baller for equal-size truffles), scoop out the chocolate and roll it gently in your hands to form the truffles. Roll them in the toppings to coat, then refrigerate until you are ready to serve.

chocolate-dipped stuffed dates

Orange-scented walnuts stuffed inside sweet dates and dipped in dark chocolate make the ultimate combination of Middle Eastern flavors in one delicious bite! These nutritious treats are quick and easy to prepare, and are a delicious way to end any meal or to satisfy a midday sweet craving.

We strongly recommend using Medjool dates for this recipe, since they are larger and easier to stuff. Store them in an airtight container in the refrigerator for up to a week.

Prep time: 20 minutes
Makes 15 dates

INGREDIENTS:

⅔ cup walnut halves, finely chopped

2 teaspoons pure maple syrup

Zest of 1 orange

15 Medjool dates, pitted

⅓ cup vegan chocolate chips

2 teaspoons coconut oil

Line a baking sheet or a tray with parchment or waxed paper.

Combine the chopped walnuts, maple syrup, and orange zest in a small bowl and mix well. Spoon the mixture into the dates, arrange them on the lined baking sheet, and refrigerate while you prepare the chocolate.

Place the chocolate and coconut oil in a heatproof bowl. Place the bowl over a pot of simmering water, making sure the bowl doesn't touch the water. Stir until the chocolate has melted. Remove the bowl from the heat and let the chocolate cool for 5 minutes. Alternatively, melt the chocolate in a microwave, at 20-second intervals on standard power until completely melted, making sure to stir well each time (this will prevent the chocolate from seizing).

Once the chocolate has cooled slightly, dip the dates about halfway though. Place them back on the lined baking sheet and refrigerate them until the chocolate has hardened or you are ready to serve them.

pomegranate, apricot, and salted cashew chocolate bark

When we were kids, our dad traveled the world on business. Sometimes he would be gone for weeks, which was difficult for us, but the one highlight was that he would always bring us treats from every corner of the planet, especially the Middle East. Salted cashews were one of our favorites, since they weren't common in Spain. Another was *amardine*, a sweet and tangy apricot paste similar to fruit leather.

These two treats are the inspiration for this sweet and savory bark. The combination of the richness of dark chocolate, the freshness of pomegranate seeds, and the salty crunch of cashews creates a dessert perfect for any festive occasion. Store in the refrigerator in an airtight container for up to a week.

Prep time: 20 minutes
Cook time: 5 minutes
Makes 10 servings

INGREDIENTS:

20 ounces vegan semisweet chocolate chunks

¾ cup dried apricots, chopped

¾ cup fresh pomegranate seeds, well patted dry

¾ cup salted cashews, roughly chopped or halved

1 teaspoon coarse sea salt (optional)

EQUIPMENT:

Parchment paper

Place the chocolate chunks in a large, heatproof glass bowl.

Fill a medium-size saucepan halfway with water and bring it to a boil over high heat. Lower the heat to a simmer and place the bowl of chocolate over the saucepan, making sure the boiling water doesn't touch the bottom of the bowl. Let the chocolate melt, stirring frequently. Alternatively, melt the chocolate in a microwave, at 20-second intervals on standard power until completely melted, making sure to stir well each time (this will prevent the chocolate from seizing).

In the meantime, line two 9 by 13-inch baking sheets with parchment paper.

Combine the dried apricots and pomegranate seeds in a bowl and set aside.

Pour half of the melted chocolate onto each lined baking sheet and spread evenly with a spatula. Sprinkle half of the dried apricots, pomegranate seeds, and cashews on top of one chocolate layer, pressing gently with the palm of your hand. Repeat the process atop the remaining chocolate on the other baking sheet.

If using, sprinkle ½ teaspoon of coarse sea salt on top of each sheet. Refrigerate until the chocolate hardens. Break into uneven pieces.

black and white tahini cookies

These melt-in-your-mouth treats are our fun take on the classic black and white cook-ie, using crunchy, rich sesame seeds for the "icing." We learned how to make tahini cookies from our sister Rebeca, who lives in Israel and is a phenomenal baker. She also has direct access to our grandmother's baking secrets!

These cookies are very delicate, so it's important that you let them cool com-pletely on the baking tray before touching them. They can be stored in an airtight container for up to a week or in the freezer for up to three months.

Prep time: 10 minutes
Cook time: 22 minutes
Makes 14 cookies

INGREDIENTS:

1 cup whole wheat pastry flour

1 cup almond flour

½ cup confectioners' sugar

½ teaspoon baking powder

⅛ teaspoon salt

½ cup tahini

¼ cup grapeseed or avocado oil

¼ cup pure maple syrup

7 teaspoons raw sesame seeds

7 teaspoons black sesame seeds

EQUIPMENT:

Parchment paper

Preheat the oven to 325°F. Line a large baking sheet with parchment paper. Place the maple syrup in a small bowl and set it aside along with a pastry brush.

Combine the wheat and almond flours, sugar, baking powder, and salt in a large bowl. Add the tahini and oil and mix well.

Using a 1½-tablespoon ice-cream scoop, scoop out fourteen dough balls and place them on the lined baking sheet. Lightly press them down, using the palm of your hand.

Brush each cookie with maple syrup and cover half of the top with white sesame seeds and the other half with black sesame seeds.

Bake for 22 minutes, or until the edges start to brown slightly, remove from the oven, and let cool completely.

melt-away moroccan cinnamon cookies

These cookies are extremely easy to prepare and practically foolproof—perfect for anyone who has trouble baking! The recipe yields a large amount of cookies—which means extra cookies that can be frozen for up to three months.

We love to serve them with Turkish coffee or espresso. Store them in an airtight container for up to a week.

Prep time: 10 minutes
Cook time: 20 minutes
Makes 4 dozen

INGREDIENTS:

1 cup neutral-flavor oil (such as sunflower, grapeseed, or avocado)

1⅓ cups confectioners' sugar

2 cups almond flour

2 cups whole wheat pastry flour

1 tablespoon ground cinnamon, plus more for sprinkling

½ teaspoon baking powder

¼ teaspoon salt

EQUIPMENT:

Parchment paper

Preheat the oven to 325°F and line two large cookie sheets with parchment paper.

Combine the oil and confectioners' sugar in a large bowl. Mix well until the sugar has dissolved. Add the almond flour and mix well.

In a separate bowl, combine the flour, cinnamon, baking powder, and salt. Add to the almond flour mixture. Mix with a wooden spoon first, then with your hands, to form a dough.

Using your hands or a small ice-cream scoop and working with 2 teaspoons of dough at a time, form forty-eight balls. Place them ½ inch apart on the lined cookie sheets and slightly flatten each ball with the palm of your hand.

Bake for 20 minutes, or until they start to firm up slightly, remove from the oven, and sprinkle cinnamon on top of each cookie. Let cool completely.

maamoul

These buttery orange blossom–scented, nut-filled semolina cookies are another of the treats we grew up eating. And it's another recipe we tried to get from our grandmother for years! But we never did because, well, she never followed one. "You have to feel the dough and you'll know if it has the right consistency," she tells us. After many tries, and with the help of the owner of a local Lebanese restaurant, we were finally able to figure out what she meant: the dough has to be soft and smooth, so it can be handled without it tearing or falling apart.

Traditional *maamoul* require a special mold (which is found easily online) to create the right shape. If you don't have one or don't want to buy it, you can follow all the steps on the recipe and simply flatten the dough with your hands after it has been filled and rolled into balls.

Store the cookies in an airtight container for up to a week, or freeze for up to three months.

Prep time: 45 minutes
Cook time: 20 minutes
Makes 16 to 18 cookies

INGREDIENTS:

1⅓ cups semolina flour

⅓ cup all-purpose flour

¼ cup granulated sugar

⅔ cup coconut oil, at room temperature

¼ cup unsweetened nondairy milk

2 tablespoons orange blossom water

1 cup shelled pistachios, coarsely ground

2 tablespoons pure maple syrup or agave nectar

Confectioners' sugar, for sprinkling

EQUIPMENT:

Parchment paper

Maamoul mold

In a large bowl, combine the semolina, flour, granulated sugar, and coconut oil. Mix well, using your hands, until the coconut oil is well incorporated (the mixture should look like coarse cornmeal at this point).

Slowly add the nondairy milk and 1 tablespoon of the orange blossom water and keep working it with your hands until it forms a smooth dough. Set aside and let rest for 20 to 25 minutes.

Meanwhile, preheat the oven to 350°F. Line a large baking sheet with parchment paper and set aside.

While the dough is resting, prepare the filling: Combine the ground pistachios, maple syrup, and remaining tablespoon of orange blossom water in a bowl and mix well.

Working with about 1½ tablespoons of dough at a time, form sixteen to eighteen balls. Using your thumb, press a wide depression into the center of each ball. Place 1 heaping teaspoon of filling in each depression, close it up, and reroll the dough into a ball.

Press each filled ball gently into the *maamoul* mold and bang the mold against the counter to release it.

Arrange the molded dough ½ inch apart on the lined baking sheet.

If you are not using a mold, place the balls ½ inch apart on the lined baking sheet and gently press so they flatten.

Bake at 350°F for 20 minutes, or until golden brown. Remove from the oven, let cool, and sprinkle with confectioners' sugar.

pistachio "nicecream" with halvah sauce

If you are an ice cream lover, you are going to love this recipe. It's not only the easiest homemade ice cream you'll ever make, it's also the healthiest! "Nicecream" is simply frozen bananas, blended until they become soft and creamy. You can add your favorite ingredients to it, such as chocolate chips, coconut, nuts, or nut butters, and also choose your favorite toppings. We are topping ours with a decadent cardamom-scented halvah sauce.

We recommend slicing the bananas and storing them in individual bags before freezing them. They will blend better in pieces, and it will help you measure how many bananas you're using.

Nicecream should be prepared right before serving. It can be frozen once it's prepared, but take into consideration that it will harden significantly and will need a few minutes out of the freezer to soften.

Prep time: 5 minutes
Makes 2 servings

INGREDIENTS:

3 bananas, sliced and frozen

¼ cup unsweetened vanilla nondairy milk

3 to 4 tablespoons shelled pistachios

½ teaspoon pure vanilla extract

HALVAH SAUCE:

3 tablespoons tahini

2 tablespoons pure maple syrup

1 tablespoon confectioners' sugar

⅛ teaspoon ground cardamom

2 tablespoons unsweetened vanilla nondairy milk

To prepare the nicecream, combine the frozen bananas, nondairy milk, pistachios, and vanilla in a food processor and pulse until you reach a creamy, ice cream–like consistency. Scoop the mixture into two bowls and place them in the freezer while you make the halvah sauce.

Prepare the halvah sauce: Whisk together all the sauce ingredients, except the milk, in a medium-size bowl, until well combined. Slowly add the nondairy milk, whisking constantly, until smooth and creamy. Spoon over the nicecream.

date and orange blossom palmiers

Palmiers are delicious sweet puff pastry treats of French Algerian origin. They are impressive to look at and to eat! Palmiers are traditionally rolled in sugar and baked until crispy and caramelized. Our version adds dates, walnuts, orange blossom water, and cinnamon to the buttery pastry, for a Middle Eastern touch.

Prep time: 45 minutes
Cook time: 17 minutes
Makes 40 palmiers

INGREDIENTS:

15 Medjool dates, pitted

½ cup walnut halves

2 teaspoons orange blossom water

1 teaspoon ground cinnamon

⅛ teaspoon salt

½ cup sugar

2 vegan puff pastry sheets, thawed in the refrigerator

EQUIPMENT:

Parchment paper

Combine the dates, walnuts, orange blossom water, cinnamon, and salt in a food processor and pulse a few times until the mixture forms a thick paste. Divide into four equal portions, roll each into an 8-inch log, and transfer the logs to a plate. Set aside.

Place a large piece of parchment or waxed paper on your working surface and sprinkle 1½ teaspoons of sugar on top. Place one sheet of puff pastry (keep the other in the refrigerator in the meantime) over it, and place another piece of paper on top of the pastry (this will keep the dough from sticking to the rolling pin). Roll the pastry into a 10-inch square (see photo). Remove the top paper and sprinkle another 1½ tablespoons of sugar on top, lightly pressing it into the dough with the rolling pin.

TIPS

Make sure you are using dates that are soft. If they are slightly dry, soak them in warm water for fifteen minutes and dry them well before using them. You can store the palmiers in an airtight container for up to a week, or in the freezer for up to two months.

Place two date logs on each vertical side of the pastry sheet, about 2 inches from the edge, and flatten them slightly, using your fingers (see photo). Fold each vertical side over toward the center, so it covers the date log (see photo).

Sprinkle 1 tablespoon of sugar on top of each fold and lightly press them with the rolling pin.

Fold the sides of the pastry one more time toward the center. Sprinkle with another tablespoon of sugar and press again with the rolling pin (see photos).

If the folded sides haven't met in the middle of the pastry sheet yet, fold them one more time and sprinkle another tablespoon of sugar.

Once the sides meet in the middle, fold them on top of each other, sprinkle with 1 tablespoon of sugar, and lightly press with the rolling pin (see photo). Place the log in the freezer to chill for 15 to 20 minutes and repeat with the other pastry sheet.

When the palmiers are ready to bake, preheat the oven to 400°F. Line two baking sheets with parchment paper.

Slice each pastry into twenty pieces, about ¼ inch thick (see photo), and arrange them about an inch apart on the lined baking sheets. Sprinkle the remaining sugar on top of each piece. Bake one sheet at a time for 15 to 17 minutes, or until the bottoms turn brown.

creamy tahini cheesecake with pistachio crust and fresh pomegranate

We've been making dairy-free cheesecake for years, and we've always used dairy-free cream cheese as our base. That is until we discovered how ground, soaked cashews have the extraordinary ability to mimic pretty much every single dairy product from ricotta to cream cheese. Cashews are incredibly versatile. In this recipe, they work beautifully with the tahini (which also adds a subtle nutty flavor), and the result is a rich and creamy cheesecake. The slightly tart pomegranate seeds cut through the creaminess of the cashew and tahini base, also providing a touch of crunch. To further accentuate the Middle Eastern flavors of this luscious dessert, we make the crust with dates and pistachios.

This recipe works best when prepared in a 7-inch springform pan. You can use a bigger mold if that is what you have on hand, but take into consideration that the cheesecake will not be as tall.

The leftover cheesecake can be frozen in an airtight container for up to a month. We recommend removing the pomegranate seeds from the top before freezing.

Prep time: 1 hour 45 minutes (includes freezing time)
Makes one 7-inch cheesecake

INGREDIENTS:

2 cups raw cashews

1½ cups boiling water

1 cup plus 2 tablespoons shelled pistachios

20 pitted dates, or 10 pitted Medjool dates

½ cup plus 1 tablespoon tahini

⅓ cup pure maple syrup

3 tablespoons coconut oil, melted

3 tablespoons unsweetened nondairy milk

1 tablespoon freshly squeezed lemon juice

½ teaspoon pure vanilla extract

TOPPING:

1 cup vegan chocolate chips

2 teaspoons coconut oil

1 cup pomegranate seeds

EQUIPMENT:

7-inch springform pan

Place the cashews in a heatproof bowl. Add the boiling water. Soak for 30 minutes and then drain.

In the meantime, prepare the crust: Combine 1 cup of the pistachios, dates, and 1 tablespoon of tahini in a food processor. Pulse until well combined and transfer the mixture to a 7-inch springform pan. Press down evenly, so the mixture comes about halfway up the sides of the pan. Refrigerate until you're ready to use it.

Prepare the filling: Combine the drained cashews, ½ cup of the tahini, and the maple syrup, melted coconut oil, nondairy milk, lemon juice, and vanilla in the food processor. Pulse until smooth, scraping the sides occasionally. Transfer the mixture to a bowl and fold in the remaining 2 tablespoons of pistachios. Pour the filling over the prepared crust and freeze for 1 hour.

Remove the cheesecake from the freezer and refrigerate until ready to serve.

Right before serving, prepare the chocolate topping: Place the chocolate chips and coconut oil in a medium-size, heatproof glass bowl. Fill a medium-size saucepan halfway with water and bring to a boil over high heat. Lower the heat to simmer and place the bowl of chocolate over the saucepan, making sure the boiling water doesn't touch the bottom of the bowl. Let the chocolate melt, stirring frequently. Alternatively, melt the chocolate in a microwave, at 20-second intervals on standard power until completely melted, making sure to stir well each time (this will prevent the chocolate from seizing).

Drizzle the melted chocolate on top of the cheesecake. Garnish with fresh pomegranate seeds.

pomegranate, almonds, and pistachios in rose water

This aromatic fruit and nut salad is a wonderful combination of textures and flavors. The almonds, walnuts, pine nuts, and pistachios become soft after being soaked in water. The almost creamy texture complements the crunch and freshness of the pomegranate seeds beautifully, and the sweet, floral rose water "broth" brings all the flavors together. Our mom used to serve this refreshing and light dessert after festive meals. It also makes a delicious midafternoon snack!

If you prefer a less prominent floral taste, reduce the amount of rose water by half.

Prep time: 4 hours
Makes 6 to 8 servings

INGREDIENTS:

½ cup raw whole almonds

½ cup raw walnut halves

¼ cup raw pine nuts

¼ cup raw shelled pistachios

¼ cup plus 1 tablespoon sugar

1 tablespoon rose water

⅓ cup pomegranate seeds

Soak the almonds, walnuts, pine nuts, and pistachios in water, in four separate bowls, for 3 to 4 hours.

Drain and discard the soaking water. Remove the almond skins, using your hands.

Combine the sugar and 2 cups of water in a large bowl. Stir well, until the sugar dissolves. Add the rose water, soaked nuts, and pomegranate seeds. Refrigerate until you are ready to serve it. Serve cold.

POMEGRANATE, ALMONDS, AND
PISTACHIOS IN ROSE WATER

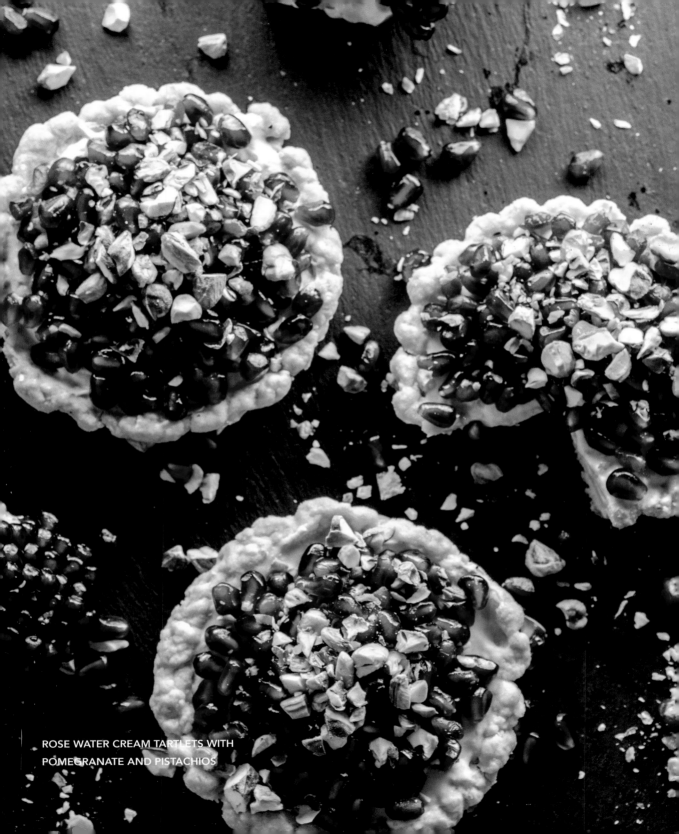

ROSE WATER CREAM TARTLETS WITH
POMEGRANATE AND PISTACHIOS

rose water cream tartlets with pomegranate and pistachios

These beautiful tartlets are our interpretation of *malabi*, a dessert of Turkish origin. This creamy pudding is eaten throughout the Middle East, and each country has its own version. We've combined both the Lebanese (which uses chopped pistachios) and Israeli (which is made with almond milk) variations, to highlight our multicultural background.

Prep time: 50 minutes
Cook time: 40 minutes
Makes 4 tartlets

INGREDIENTS:

SHORTBREAD:

Cooking spray

½ cup coconut oil

1 tablespoon granulated sugar

2 tablespoons confectioners' sugar

½ teaspoon pure vanilla extract

1 cup all-purpose flour

⅛ teaspoon salt

2 tablespoons unflavored coconut creamer

ROSE WATER CREAM:

1½ cups unflavored coconut creamer

2 tablespoons cornstarch

2 tablespoons pure maple syrup

1 tablespoon rose water

1 teaspoon pure vanilla extract

2 tablespoons coconut oil

1 cup pomegranate seeds

¼ cup shelled roasted pistachios

EQUIPMENT:

4 (4-inch) tartlet molds

> TIP
>
> The shortbread crust can be prepared two to three days in advance and stored in the refrigerator. Once the tartlets are filled with the cream, we recommend keeping them in the refrigerator for no more than a day, since the cream might start to crack.

To prepare the shortbread: Preheat the oven to 350°F. Coat four 4-inch tartlet molds with cooking spray and set aside.

In a medium-size bowl and using an electric mixer, cream together the coconut oil and granulated sugar for 1 minute. Add the confectioners' sugar and vanilla and continue to beat for another minute until combined.

Reduce the speed of the mixer. Add the flour, salt, and creamer and mix until just incorporated.

Using your hands, pull the mix together to form a dough.

Divide the dough into four equal pieces. Press each piece into a prepared tartlet mold, as evenly as possible, so it slightly comes up the sides. Refrigerate for 15 minutes.

Prick the dough with a fork several times (this will prevent it from bubbling up) and bake for 25 to 30 minutes, or until lightly golden. Set aside to cool completely.

Prepare the rose water cream: Whisk the cornstarch into ½ cup of the creamer in a small bowl, making sure the cornstarch dissolves completely. Set it aside.

Combine the remaining cup of creamer and the maple syrup in a small saucepan and whisk well. Place over medium heat and simmer for 6 to 7 minutes.

Pour the cornstarch mixture into the warm creamer and continue to cook for 2 minutes, whisking constantly, until it thickens.

Remove the saucepan from the heat and whisk in the rose water and vanilla extract. Add the coconut oil and mix well until it melts completely. Transfer to a bowl and let cool at room temperature for 25 to 30 minutes. The mixture will thicken as it cools.

> TIP
>
> The cream has a prominent rose water flavor. If you have never had rose water, or prefer a milder taste, start with 2 teaspoons, taste it, and add more if necessary.

To assemble the tarts, remove the shortbread from the tart molds and place them on a serving plate. Spoon the rose water cream into each tartlet, and top each with ¼ cup of pomegranate seeds and 1 tablespoon of pistachios. Refrigerate for at least 1 hour, or until you are ready to serve them.

candied spaghetti squash and pine nut tart

Our mom is an amazing cook, but she's the first to admit that she's not much of a baker.

She has a few standout specialties, though: this somewhat unusual tart is one of them. If you've eaten spaghetti squash in savory dishes, you know it also contains some sweetness. That sweetness is highlighted here, offset by rich pine nuts. In Spain, you can find the filling already prepared in jars at the grocery store, so Mami just added orange blossom water, spread it on a sheet of puff pastry, and done!

Elsewhere, however, this dessert is slightly more time consuming, since the filling has to be prepared from scratch. But since it freezes really well, you can prepare a large batch, portion it, freeze it, and thaw just what you need.

Prep time: 1 hour
Cook time: 2 hours
Makes 2 tarts; serves 9 per tart

INGREDIENTS:

1 medium-size spaghetti squash

1 cup water

1 cup plus 2 tablespoons sugar

1 tablespoon freshly squeezed lemon juice

2 teaspoons orange blossom water (optional)

2 sheets vegan puff pastry, thawed

1 cup pine nuts

¼ cup unsweetened nondairy milk, for brushing

EQUIPMENT:
Parchment paper

Preheat the oven to 400°F and line a large baking sheet with parchment paper. Cut the spaghetti squash in half lengthwise. Scoop out and discard the seeds. Place both halves, cut side down, on the lined baking sheet and bake for 45 minutes, or until soft. Remove from the oven and let cool completely, about 20 minutes. Scoop out the flesh, using a fork (this should yield about 2¼ cups). Squeeze out any excess water.

Combine 1 cup of water and 1 cup of the sugar in a saucepan. Bring to a boil over high heat, whisking constantly to dissolve the sugar. Add the lemon juice and spaghetti squash. Return to a boil, lower the heat to medium, and cook for 50 minutes to an hour, stirring occasionally, or until all the water has evaporated. Remove from the heat and let cool completely, 30 to 40 minutes. Add the orange blossom water, if using, and mix well.

Preheat the oven to 375°F. Line a large baking sheet with parchment paper.

Roll out each puff pastry sheet into a 9-inch square. Lightly score a 1-inch border along all sides.

Spread 1 heaping cup of candied spaghetti squash over each pastry sheet. Evenly sprinkle with ½ cup of pine nuts, pushing them lightly into the candied spaghetti squash and sprinkle 1 tablespoon of the remaining sugar on top of each tart. Brush the border with nondairy milk.

Bake for 25 minutes, or until golden brown. Serve warm.

coconut turmeric sweet bread (*sfuff*)

This aromatic, nutty sweet bread has a pronounced turmeric taste and a crumbly texture, thanks to the unsweetened shredded coconut. It's also one of the simplest, most delicious cakes you'll ever make. Mixing turmeric with baking powder and baking soda turns the cake red (not yellow!) once it's baked. Oddly enough, that doesn't happen when self-rising flour is used and the baking powder is omitted. If you don't have self-rising flour at home, you can use all-purpose flour and add 2½ teaspoons of baking powder. Just remember that the cake will have little red specks instead of being completely yellow! Store in an airtight container for up to a week, or in the freezer for up to a month.

Prep time: 10 minutes
Cook time: 30 minutes
Makes one 8-inch-square cake

INGREDIENTS:

1 tablespoon tahini, for baking dish

1½ cups self-rising flour

¾ cup unsweetened shredded coconut

½ cup sugar

1 tablespoon ground turmeric

⅛ teaspoon salt

¾ cup unsweetened nondairy milk, lukewarm

½ cup coconut oil, melted

8 to 10 shelled pistachios, for garnish (optional)

Preheat the oven to 350°F. Using your fingers, spread a thin layer of tahini on the bottom and sides of an 8-inch square baking dish. Set aside.

Combine the flour, coconut, sugar, turmeric, and salt in a large bowl.

In a separate bowl, whisk together the lukewarm nondairy milk and melted coconut oil. Pour the milk mixture over the flour mixture and mix, using a wooden spoon, until the ingredients are just combined (the batter will be very thick, almost like a very soft dough). Transfer to the tahini-coated baking dish, top with the shelled pistachios, and bake for 25 to 30 minutes, or until a toothpick inserted into the center comes out clean.

COCONUT TURMERIC
SWEET BREAD (*SFUFF*)

SEMOLINA-STUFFED KATAIFI NESTS
WITH ORANGE BLOSSOM SYRUP

semolina-stuffed kataifi nests with orange blossom syrup

Kataifi is shredded phyllo dough that is used in many Greek and Middle Eastern dishes, both sweet and savory. It has a wonderful, light crunch once it's baked. It's usually sold frozen, so you will need to thaw it in the refrigerator before using it. It can be found online on Amazon.com or in Middle Eastern stores.

Because it dries easily, we recommend covering the kataifi with a damp towel when you are not working with it. Our nests are filled with an orange blossom– and rose water–infused semolina custard and drizzled with a citrusy orange blossom syrup.

The baked nests can be frozen for up to a month. To reheat them, let them thaw and then place them in a 300°F oven for ten minutes, or until they crisp up again.

Prep time: 1 hour and 15 minutes
Cook time: 35 minutes
Makes 12 nests

INGREDIENTS:

2 cups unsweetened nondairy milk

½ cup semolina flour

¼ cup sugar

1 teaspoon rose water

1 teaspoon orange blossom water

4 cups packed kataifi, thawed

⅓ cup refined coconut oil, melted, plus more for pan

½ cup chopped pistachios

ORANGE BLOSSOM SYRUP:

½ cup sugar

1½ teaspoons freshly squeezed lemon juice

1 teaspoon orange blossom water

EQUIPMENT:

12-well muffin tin

Prepare the filling: Combine the nondairy milk, semolina, sugar, rose water, and orange blossom water in a medium-size saucepan and whisk well. Cook over medium heat for 3 to 4 minutes, or until the mixture thickens, whisking often. Refrigerate the filling until you are ready to use it.

Preheat the oven to 375°F. Generously grease a 12-well muffin tin with coconut oil.

Place the kataifi in a bowl and separate the strands with your hands. Pour in the coconut oil and mix well until the strands are well coated.

Place a heaping ¼ cup of kataifi in each prepared muffin well, pressing down so it comes up the sides to form a nest. Spoon 2 tablespoons of the cooled filling inside each nest. Bake for 20 minutes, or until golden brown.

While the nests are in the oven, prepare the syrup: Combine the sugar and ¼ cup of water in a small saucepan and cook over medium heat for 2 to 3 minutes, until the sugar has dissolved completely. Add the lemon juice and orange blossom water, lower the heat, and simmer for 5 minutes. Set aside until you are ready to use it.

Remove the nests from the oven and let cool until safe to handle. Carefully remove them from the muffin tin by sliding a butter knife around the edges. Drizzle with orange blossom syrup while they're still warm, and top with chopped pistachios.

CANDIED SPAGHETTI SQUASH
AND PINE NUT TART

acknowledgments

We are incredibly grateful to our family, friends, and readers for the unconditional love and support that have made the creation of this cookbook possible. And to our recipe testers, Megan, Cindy F., Cindy M., Raquel, Susan, Karen, and Shani, for taking the time to help us out and for your valuable feedback.

A very special, heartfelt thank-you to:

Our parents, Mami and Papi, our sister Rebeca, and our grandmother Abuelita. "Thank you" doesn't begin to express our gratitude and appreciation. We are so thankful for the inspiration, your support, and your unconditional love. And for instilling in us the passion and appreciation for good food and cooking.

To Lee, Raquel, Zeke, Haim, Netanel, Lior, Mike, and Solly, who volunteered to taste our culinary creations over and over and never complained. Thank you for cheering us on through the journey of creating this cookbook.

Our dear friend and "adopted sister" Megan. For being our number one fan from the beginning. For your unconditional support and for believing in us when we couldn't believe in ourselves. And most of all, for having the warmest, biggest heart of anyone we know.

Phyllis, Zachary, Jeff, and Sophie, for being our biggest cheerleaders; for your contagious excitement, and for always being there to boost our confidence when we need it.

Dianne Jacob, our amazing coach and literary genius, for guiding us through this journey and pushing us through the uphills. Thank you for believing in us.

Our life coach, Cindy Faust, for guiding us, keeping us grounded and focused, and believing in us and our vision from the very beginning.

To our friend Cindy McFee, thank you for always being with us, inspiring us with your endless energy, and for your unwavering enthusiasm. Your help is truly invaluable.

To my (Vicky's) husband, Lee, for allowing me the opportunity to follow my dreams over and over again, for inspiring me to grow, and for teaching me self-discovery. You make life's ups and downs easier with your care and love; it is a ride I would only want to take with you.

To Herb and Naomi, thank you for your insightful guidance and advice. Your unparalleled generosity is appreciated more than we can express.

To our dear friend Robert Cohen, for your valuable legal advice and for making our Friday night dinners more enjoyable.

To our talented friend Nicole, at Nicole Graziano Photography, for taking our portrait shots and making our photoshoot easy and fun. And especially for making two very shy girls feel comfortable in front of the camera.

To our agent Coleen O'Shea, for the enthusiasm you showed the moment we came to you with this project, for your patience, and, most of all, for your encouragement and guidance.

To our wonderful editor, Renée Sedliar, for your incredible kindness, enthusiasm, and patience while guiding us through writing this cookbook. To our project editors Julia Campbell and Michael Clark, copyeditor Iris Bass, and designers Kerry Rubenstein and Nancy Singer, for being so thorough and creative. We are honestly amazed by the work you do!

index

index

about the authors

Vicky Cohen and Ruth Fox

maylhavethatrecipe.com

Start with a dash of Spain, a chunk of Lebanon, a splash of Israel, and a hint of America. Blend until smooth, and voilà! You may end up with a well-mixed identity crisis, but for the most part, you'll get Vicky and Ruth: two sisters raised in Barcelona by Syrian-Lebanese Jewish parents, now living in New Jersey.

Recipe developers, cooking instructors, and food enthusiasts, Vicky and Ruth are the creators of the standout food blog MayIHaveThatRecipe.com. Vicky and Ruth have worked with Food.com, GO Veggie!, Natural & Kosher, and Sincerely Brigitte and have developed recipes for companies such as Explore Cuisine, Silk, Colavita, Maille, So Delicious, Gold's, Olive Oils of Spain, Sabra, and others. Their recipes have been featured on many different websites, including Buzzfeed Food, Whole Foods, HuffingtonPost.com, *Shape* magazine, *Redbook*, Serious Eats, PETA, Greatist, and Brit+Co.